Thomas Gaisford

Regius Professor of Greek and a Curator of the Bodleian Library, 1812–1855.

R. W. Hunt and others

The Survival of Ancient Literature

Catalogue
of
an exhibition
of Greek and Latin classical manuscripts
mainly from Oxford libraries
displayed
on the occasion of
the Triennial Meeting of the Hellenic and Roman Societies
28 July – 2 August 1975.

Bodleian Library
OXFORD
1975

Front cover: no. 124. Philosophy appears to Boethius in prison.   MS. Auct. F.6.5, fol. 1ᵛ.

Back cover: no. 55. Euclid, Elements, end of Bk. XI, with alternative diagrams for
          proposition 39.   MS. D'Orville 301, fol. 305.

Frontispiece: Thomas Gaisford. A mezzotint by T. L. Atkinson, published in 1848,
          here reproduced by courtesy of the Visitors of the Ashmolean Museum;
          after the original portrait by H. W. Pickersgill, now at Christ Church.

Printed by TRUExpress Oxford.

CONTENTS

FOREWORD

At the end of September 1975 Dr. Richard Hunt retires, under the age limit, from the Keepership of Western Manuscripts which he has held since 1945 and thus brings to an end a period of office of rare distinction in the history of the Bodleian Library.

In the course of this time the Library's manuscript collections have grown remarkably and have been greatly diversified. In addition to acquiring, in spite of their ascending prices, further medieval and Renaissance manuscripts — the area of Bodley's traditional greatness — we have added many literary manuscripts extending in time from Donne to Masefield; musical manuscripts of some of the greatest composers; historical documents from the memoirs of Ludlow to the personal papers of Cabinet Ministers of this century; business archives from the books of seventeenth-century stonemasons to files of correspondence of contemporary publishers. In all these fields the Library's policy has been shaped by Dr. Hunt's energy, vision, and initiative, and we had thought to mark his retirement with an exhibition of acquisitions made during his Keepership.

Another idea, however, better and intellectually more satisfying, was proposed by Dr. Hunt himself: that an exhibition should be mounted on the specific theme of the survival and transmission of classical texts. This is the subject which par excellence is his own, in which his teaching has been concentrated and in which he has made his major contributions to scholarship. We are glad to put on this exhibition at the time of the triennial meeting of the Greek and Roman Societies in Oxford. It is intended to commemorate one of the most illustrious stewardships the Bodleian Library has known.

Robert Shackleton
Bodley's Librarian

iv

PREFACE

We are grateful to many Oxford Colleges, Balliol, Christ Church, Corpus Christi, Exeter, Lincoln, Merton, New, Queen's, St. John's and Trinity, for allowing us to draw on their collections. We are also grateful to the Provost and Fellows of Eton College for lending a famous Beneventan manuscript (no. 114). The Egypt Exploration Society has put us greatly in its debt by allowing us to borrow Latin papyri which have never before been exhibited and which have greatly extended our range in illustrating the ancient Latin book. R.A. Coles has kindly mounted these papyri for us.

In the choice of plates we have concentrated on manuscripts which have not been reproduced before. The plates of Latin manuscripts outnumber the Greek, since N.G. Wilson has recently published Mediaeval Greek bookhands (Mediaeval Academy of America. Publication no. 81), Cambridge (Mass.) 1973, an album drawn from the Bodleian collections. We have extended the length of the catalogue entries when there are new things to be said.

The section on Greek manuscripts is the work of N.G. Wilson, fellow of Lincoln College and Bodleian consultant on Greek manuscripts. The entries for Latin manuscripts have been composed by B.C. Barker-Benfield, A.C. de la Mare and myself. Theirs has been the lion's share, and they have generously contributed unpublished material of their own. B.C. Barker-Benfield has been responsible for the arrangement of the exhibits as well as for writing out the catalogue in his own hand. G.M. Briggs has given much help by looking over the catalogue with her usual ἀκρίβεια. C. Starks has also provided help in many ways. Finally we should like to thank Mrs. H. Jenkins of Truexpress for her patience and care in printing the catalogue.

R.W. Hunt
Keeper of Western Manuscripts.

INTRODUCTION

Apart from a few stars such as the Clarke Plato (no. 56) and the Catullus (no. 141), important manuscripts of major classical authors are poorly represented in Oxford libraries. To make intelligible the story of the transmission of ancient literature, we have therefore extended our range to include late antique authors, whom the purist might not consider 'classical', and some Christian writers. There are also exhibits illustrating the use made of certain works by medieval and Renaissance scholars, or their work on the texts. Thanks to the College libraries, our range of English manuscripts is especially strong; the role which England played in the transmission of texts after its eighth-century glory is a modest one, but worthy of study.

When the Bodleian Library was opened to readers on 8 November 1602, it possessed a working collection of printed books and over 250 manuscripts, which Sir Thomas Bodley and his first librarian, Thomas James, had been gathering together. Two of the foundation manuscripts are included in this exhibition, the 10th-cent. Persius (no. 118) which had come from the Dean and Chapter of Exeter, and the 9th-cent. Ovid (no. 117), the gift of Thomas Allen of Gloucester Hall.

There was no reserve of Carolingian manuscripts in English monastic libraries comparable to those in France and Germany which came to enrich the splendid collections of classical manuscripts now in Paris, Munich and the Vatican. But thanks to the efforts of William Laud, archbishop of Canterbury and chancellor of the University, something came the way of Oxford. It was he who encouraged William Herbert, 3rd earl of Pembroke and his predecessor as chancellor, to purchase and present Giacomo Barocci's collection of Greek manuscripts. Laud's own donations included important Greek and Latin manuscripts. One of his earlier acquisitions was a group of manuscripts from an unidentified French collection, among them the Martianus Capella (no. 100). Between 1636 and 1638 he bought, largely from Germany, manuscripts that had been thrown onto the markets by the disturbances of war. These included a group from the Cistercian monastery of Eberbach, some of which had come there from the great Carolingian abbey of Lorsch (nos. 96, 98).

The first collection of classical manuscripts acquired for the Library was that bought by Edward Bernard at the sale of Nicholas Heinsius at Leiden in 1683, and, in accordance with his wish, bought by the University in 1698 after his death. Among our exhibits from this source is the Carolingian Vergil (no. 23). Soon afterwards the Library received by gift in 1704 and 1706 the two finest English illuminated books in the exhibition, the Terence (no. 127) and the Herbal (no. 122).

In the early 19th century, the Bodleian had increased resources for the purchase of books and manuscripts. It was a time when the study of the Greek and Latin classics was in honour in the University. During this period some of our greatest treasures were acquired: among the Greek manuscripts, the D'Orville Euclid (no. 55), the Clarke Plato (no. 56), and the Saibante Epictetus (no. 61), among the Latin the Canonici Juvenal (no. 113) and Catullus (no. 141). The collection of Jacques Philippe D'Orville was purchased in 1804, of E. D. Clarke in 1809, of the Abate Matteo Luigi Canonici in 1817. A group of 50 Greek manuscripts from the Saibante collection was purchased in 1820, and extensive purchases were made at the sale in 1824 of the Meerman collection, which incorporated the manuscripts of the Jesuit College of Clermont in Paris, acquired in 1764 by Gerarard Meerman after the college's dissolution. There does not seem to be evidence to show who initiated this series of purchases, but Thomas Gaisford (1779-1855) was early concerned and carried on the movement. He must have started work on the catalogue of D'Orville manuscripts as soon as they were acquired, since it was published in 1806. He followed it with a catalogue of the Clarke manuscripts in 1812. In that year he became Regius Professor of Greek and hence ex officio a Curator of the Bodleian. In 1824 he went over to the Hague in person to bid at the Meerman sale and succeeded in buying many important classical manuscripts, in spite of the interference of a 'meddling baronet', Sir Thomas Phillipps. An onlooker after the sale observed 'the Greek Professor standing without his coat and his hands clasped, so anxious in overlooking the packing, without being able to render any actual assistance'. The chief prize, not fully recognized until 1889, was the 5th-cent. Eusebius (no. 34). Gaisford can fairly be called the hero of this exhibition, and for this reason we have chosen his portrait as a frontispiece.

In the later 19th and in the present century, opportunities to acquire Latin and Greek classical manuscripts have become increasingly rare. Nevertheless, there has been one major accession: the 108 Greek manuscripts, purchased with the generous help of the Dulverton Trust from the Earl of Leicester's library at Holkham Hall in 1954, included a number of classical texts. Among Latin manuscripts from the same source are the Caesar (no. 91) and the important Propertius (no. 144). Miscellaneous purchases include the 'Codex Ashmolensis', Bartolomeo Fonzio's epigraphical collection (no. 149), bought as recently as 1964.

List of abbreviations

held in connection with the XIIIth International Congress of Byzantine Studies, 1966.

Exh. Duke Humfrey 1970. [A.C. de la Mare & R.W. Hunt], *Duke Humfrey and English humanism in the fifteenth century. Catalogue of an exhibition*…, Bodleian Library Oxford, 1970.

Exh. Ital. Hum. 1974. [A.C. de la Mare], *Autographs of Italian humanists. An exhibition to mark the visit of the Association Internationale de Bibliophilie* …, Bodleian Library Oxford, 1974.

Exh. Pap. 1974. [J.R. Rea], *An exhibition of papyri, mainly in Greek, at the Bodleian Library and at the Ashmolean Museum, for the XIV International Congress of Papyrologists* …, 1974.

Pächt & Alexander. O. Pächt & J.J.G. Alexander, *Illuminated manuscripts in the Bodleian Library Oxford*, 3 vols, and separate concordance of Bodleian shelfmarks, Oxford 1966–74.

Wilson. N.G. Wilson, *Mediaeval Greek bookhands (Mediaeval Academy of America. Publications no. 81)*, Cambridge (Mass.), 1973.

Homer & Vergil

1-11. Papyri of Homer

Homer appears in the papyri far more frequently than any other author. Copies of the Odyssey (see no. 7) are much less common than those of the Iliad, being out-numbered by something like four to one. The Bodleian collections offer a representative sample of Homeric papyri ranging from the 3rd cent. B.C. to the 7th cent. A.D.

1. Fragments of Iliad XXI–XXIII.   3rd cent. B.C.

This book was recovered from cartonnage (the material made of waste papyrus for mummy cases), which has proved a rich source of literary texts.

Literary papyri of this early date are by no means common, and this one has the added interest of being one of the best examples of what are sometimes called the 'wild' or 'eccentric' papyri of Homer. The text deviates substantially, e.g. by the omission or addition of whole lines, from the standard version later established by the Alexandrian scholars.

Bibl.: P.Grenf. II 4 (bought from B.P. Grenfell in 1896) + P. Hibeh 22 (given by the Egypt Exploration Fund in 1909). Other fragments are in Heidelberg, Universitätsbibliothek (P. Heidelberg 1262–6). Pack² no. 979. For a full discussion, see S.R. West, The Ptolemaic papyri of Homer (Papyrologica Coloniensia, 3), Cologne 1967, 136–191.

MS. Gr. class. b. 3 (P)/2 (part of the second of four frames)

2. Fragment of APOLLONIUS the Sophist, Lexicon Homericum.

From an ancient monograph on Homeric vocabulary.   1st cent. A.D.

Later history: bought from B. P. Grenfell in 1895.

Bibl.: published by E. W. B. Nicholson in *Classical Review* 11 (1897), 390-3. Pack² no. 1217. N. G. Hammond &

   H. H. Scullard, eds., *The Oxford Classical Dictionary*, 2nd ed., Oxford 1970, 86 (gives further bibliography).

<u>MS. Gr. class. e. 44 (P)</u>

3. <u>Iliad</u> II.   2nd cent. A.D.

   Two frames (from a total of ten) of the so-called 'Hawara Homer', discovered
in the cemetery at Hawara by W. M. Flinders Petrie. The book was lying rolled
up under the head of a mummified woman.

   The script is a fine rounded capital hand of large size. In the left-hand margin
of frame 10 there are some critical signs of the type developed by the Alexandrian
scholars. There are also some brief scholia in which Aristarchus (216-144 B.C.), the
greatest of the Hellenistic critics, is named.

Later history: given in 1888 by Jesse Haworth, a Lancashire manufacturer who helped to finance Petrie's excavations.

Bibl.: Pack² no. 616. Exh. Pap. 1974, no. 21. Illustrated in E. G. Turner, <u>Greek manuscripts of the ancient world</u>,

   Oxford 1971, pl. 13, and in L. D. Reynolds & N. G. Wilson, <u>Scribes and scholars</u>, 2nd ed., Oxford 1974, pl. I.

<u>MS. Gr. class. a. 1 (P)/9-10</u>

4. Fragment of <u>Iliad</u> XVII.   2nd cent. A.D.

   The text is accompanied by marginal notes on the right in a smaller but
similar hand.   *Bibl.*: P. Oxy. 685 (given in 1906). Pack² no. 950.

<u>MS. Gr. class. f. 75 (P)</u>

5. <u>Iliad</u> V.   Early 3rd cent. A.D.

   This copy is written on the verso of a petition dated A.D. 186. The fine sloping
hand is rather better than might be expected from a text written on what was

in effect waste paper.

Bibl. : P. Oxy. 223 (given in 1903). Pack² no. 733. Exh. Pap. 1974, no. 33. Illustrated in C.H. Roberts, Greek literary hands,

   Oxford 1955, pl. 21a.

<u>MS. Gr. class. a. 8 (P) / 1</u> verso (three smaller frames, a. 8(P)/2 a-c, are not shown)

6. Fragment of <u>Iliad</u> I.   3rd cent. A.D.

<u>Later history</u> : from the Fayum. Bought from B.P. Grenfell in 1895.

<u>Bibl.</u> : no. 004 in W. Lameere, <u>Aperçu de paléographie homérique</u>, Paris & Brussels 1960, pp. 255-8. Pack² no. 581.

<u>MS. Gr. class. g. 16 (P)</u>

7. Fragment of <u>Odyssey</u> V.   3rd cent. A.D.

<u>Later history</u> : from the Fayum. Bought from B.P. Grenfell in 1894.   <u>Bibl.</u> : P. Grenf. I 3. Pack² no. 1061.

<u>MS. Gr. class. g. 7 (P)</u>

8. Fragment of <u>Iliad</u> XII.   From a papyrus roll.   4th cent. A.D.

<u>Later history</u> : from the Fayum. Bought from B.P. Grenfell in 1894.   <u>Bibl.</u> : P. Grenf. I 4. Pack² no. 895.

<u>MS. Gr. class. e. 21 (P)</u>

9. Fragment of <u>Iliad</u> XVIII.   4th or 5th cent. A.D.

From a papyrus codex (there is original text on both sides).

<u>Later history</u> : from Hermopolis. Bought from B.P. Grenfell & A.S. Hunt in 1906.

<u>Bibl.</u>: Mélanges Nicole, Geneva 1905, 222-3. Pack² no. 961.

<u>MS. Gr. class. g. 49 (P)</u>

10. Notes on <u>Iliad</u> II.   6th cent. A.D.

Fragment of a vocabulary list, Homeric words on the left, synonyms on the right.
From a papyrus codex.   <u>Later history</u> : bought from B.P. Grenfell in 1895.

<u>MS. Gr. class. f. 41 (P)</u>

11. Notes on <u>Iliad</u> XI.   7th cent. A.D. (?)

Fragment from a parchment codex. It is another vocabulary list arranged in the same way as no. 10. The script is an uncial type very difficult to date precisely.

Later history: bought from B. P. Grenfell in 1895.

<u>MS. Gr. class. f. 39 (P)</u>

12-20. Manuscripts of Homer

These manuscripts illustrate the continuing popularity of Homer as the basic school text in Byzantium (nos. 12-16) and in Renaissance Italy (nos. 17-20).

12. Scholia on the <u>Odyssey</u>.   Late 10th cent.

The only early copy of the scholia minora on the <u>Odyssey</u>, with hypothesis to each book. The resemblance to nos. 10 and 11 is obvious. The hand is very likely that of Gregorios Kouboukleisios, who copied Florence, Laur., Plut. 69,6, probably in 997.

The manuscript was bought from Giovanni Aurispa by Niccolò Niccoli before 1424, and deposited with the rest of Niccoli's library in 1444 in S. Marco, Florence.

Later history: bought by the Bodleian from the booksellers Payne & Foss in 1832.

Bibl.: Coxe, <u>Greek MSS.</u>, Misc. no. 288. Exh. Byz. 1966, no. 45. B. L. Ullman & P. A. Stadter, <u>The public library</u>

<u>of Renaissance Florence</u> (Medioevo e Umanesimo 10), Padua 1972, pp. 55, 65, 79, 263-4, 279. Wilson, pl. 33.

Pages exhibited: fols. 65ᵛ-66ʳ, showing scholia on the end of Bk. VII and the beginning of Bk. VIII, with the hypothesis.

<u>MS. Auct. V. 1. 51</u>

13. <u>Iliad</u>.   Late 11th or early 12th cent.

A fine copy with plentiful marginal scholia. The script is highly individual, probably the work of private scholars rather than professional calligraphers.

Later history: Clermont → Meerman.   Bibl.: Coxe, Greek MSS., Misc. no. 207. Wilson, pls. 40–41.

Pages exhibited: fols 226ᵛ–227ʳ, the opening of Bk. XIV.

MS. Auct. T. 2. 7

14. JOHANNES TZETZES, Allegoriae Iliadis.   13th cent.

Tzetzes (c. 1110 – c. 1180) was one of the most active, though not the most intelligent, scholars of his day. He composed not only prose commentaries on Homer and other authors, e.g. Aristophanes, but also this work in verse, continuing the tradition of allegorical exegesis of Homer which had begun in the 6th cent. B.C.

Bibl.: Coxe, Greek MSS., col. 31.   Page exhibited: fol. 38ᵛ, the beginning of Tzetzes' verses on Iliad I.

MS. Barocci 24

15. Iliad, etc.   (a) 13th cent. (or earlier?). (b) early 14th cent.

This volume is probably composite, for it falls into two distinct sections. A glossing hand of the 15th cent., found in both parts, shows that they had been bound together by that time.

(a) is written on Oriental paper, and contains the Iliad.

(b) contains various commentaries: Tzetzes' paraphrase, as in no. 14; pseudo-Heraclitus, the ancient monograph on allegory; and some grammatical notes (epimerismoi) on Homeric vocabulary. The script of this section suggests that it originated in a Greek community in the extreme south of Italy, perhaps Otranto. The paper is Western, with a watermark that can be dated to c. A.D. 1326 (V. A. Mošin & S. M. Traljić, Vodeni znakovi, Zagreb 1957, no. 7260).

Later history: given by William Ferrers, 'a Turkey Merchant of London', in 1633.   Bibl.: Coxe, College MSS.

Pages exhibited: fols. 104ᵛ–105ʳ, the end of Bk. XXIII and the beginning of Bk. XXIV, in part (a).

New College, MS. 298   PLATE I

16. <u>Iliad</u> I–XII.   14th cent.

This book is of no special interest as a copy of Homer, but it contains a note at the end on fol. 182ʳ (exhibited) in the hand of the scribe, recording the collapse of the dome of Haghia Sophia on 19 May 1346.

<u>Bibl.</u>: R. Barbour in <u>B.L.R.</u>, 6 (1960), 608.

MS. Holkham Gr. 83

17. <u>Odyssey</u>.   Middle of the 15th cent.

The interlinear and marginal glosses in Latin which occasionally appear are in the hand of Pietro da Montagnana, a scholar who lived from 1457 to 1478 in the monastery of San Giovanni di Verdara in Padua. On his death, his books (Greek, Latin and Hebrew) became the property of the monastery. The hand of the Greek text is known from other manuscripts which were in Pietro's library, but the scribe remains unidentified. Fol. 7ʳ, exhibited, has two notes on the various possible spellings of the name Odysseus in Greek; the first runs 'datiuus ionicus per η, per unum s causa metri'.

<u>Later history</u>: acquired in a large group of manuscripts, including several others annotated by Pietro, from San Giovanni di Verdara by Thomas Coke (1698–1759) in 1717 (see W.O. Hassall, The Holkham Library, Roxburghe Club 1970, 23-4).

<u>Bibl.</u>: R. Barbour in <u>B.L.R.</u> 6 (1960), 608. R.W. Hunt in <u>B.L.R.</u> 9 (1973), 17-22, pl. v.

MS. Holkham Gr. 84

18. <u>Iliad</u>.   Middle of the 15th cent.

Written by a well-known Renaissance calligrapher, Michael Lyngeus or Lygizos (not signed). Interlinear glosses in carmine are written by the scribe as far as fol. 227ᵛ; the wide margins suggest that it may have been the scribe's intention to add scholia, but he did not even begin this task.

The manuscript belonged to Johann von Löffelholz of Nürnberg (1448–1509),

2115

who studied law at Padua in 1465; it was acquired from his estate in 1510 by Johann Geuder, also of Nürnberg.

The binding is Italian, 15th-cent., perhaps original.

<u>Later history</u>: given by E. P. Warren.   <u>Page exhibited</u>: fol. 183ʳ, the introduction to and opening lines of Iliad x.

<u>Corpus Christi College, MS. 470</u>

19. <u>Odyssey</u>.   Late 15th cent.

The script appears to be that of Demetrius Moschus, a well-known scribe of the Renaissance who specialised in preparing copies of Apollonius Rhodius. Fols. 268ᵛ-9ʳ, exhibited, contain the end of the <u>Odyssey</u>, followed by verses on it in a Western hand which added occasional marginalia elsewhere in the volume.

<u>Later history</u>: Soranzo 916 in folio.

<u>Bibl.</u>: G. Speake & F. Vian, in <u>Greek, Roman and Byzantine Studies</u>, 14 (1973), 314-8. Coxe, <u>Canonici MSS</u>, col. 78.

<u>MS. Canon. Gr. 79</u>

20. <u>Iliad</u>.   Late 15th cent.

A copy on parchment, which at this date had been replaced by paper in all but the most luxuriously produced books. The script is probably that of a Western humanist rather than a Greek refugee from Byzantium.

<u>Bibl.</u>: Coxe, <u>Canonici MSS</u>., col. 50.   <u>Pages exhibited</u>: fols. 36ᵛ-37ʳ, the end of Bk. II and the beginning of Bk. III.

<u>MS. Canon. Gr. 43</u>

21-29. Vergil

Vergil survives in more ancient copies, both fragments and complete codices, than any other Latin author. Our Vergil section starts with two 4th-cent. fragments from Antinoë, no. 21 from a huge luxury copy doubtless made for a collector, and no. 22 from a book which must have resembled the famous copies in rustic capitals which still survive intact (see no. 28).

Like Homer, Vergil has occupied a central place in education from ancient to modern times. The text of Vergil had already in antiquity an elaborate learned apparatus which was transmitted to the Middle Ages and of which the commentary of Servius is the best-known example (see nos. 23, 24, 112). No. 23, a 9th-cent. copy from a major French centre, has extensive annotations in contemporary and later hands, and the continued accumulation of material on Vergil is shown by the work of Pomponio Leto and his Roman Academy in the second half of the 15th cent. (nos. 26-28).

Vergil's continuing influence on later poets is illustrated by Shelley's beautiful translation of some lines from Eclogues X (no. 29). Canonici's belief that his magnificent copy of Vergil in 11th-cent. Beneventan script (no. 112) had belonged to the Alighieri family and hence could have been 'Dante's Vergil', has no earlier evidence to confirm it.

21. Fragment of Georgics (II.527 – III.25).   4th cent. A.D.

The papyrus codex represented by these poor scraps from a single leaf was once a book of great magnificence. The side shown (recto) contains the end of Georgics II, followed by the closing title of Bk. II and the opening title of Bk. III in red, and a short introduction to Bk. III. The first three lines of Bk. III on the verso are also in red. The main text is written in a 'stately bd-uncial' and the introduction in a smaller 'mixed half-uncial' (E.A. Lowe).

The complete page cannot have measured less than 41 x 27.5 cm., the largest size for a papyrus codex yet discovered, and the use of red ink for titles etc. is the earliest known. Most fragments of Vergil found in Egypt are schoolroom texts of the Aeneid, but this fragment of the Georgics (a text rare among the finds) must be from a collector's luxury copy — a theory not incompatible with its poor textual quality.

Later history: excavated at Antinoë in 1913–14. Now kept at the Ashmolean Museum.

Bibl.: P. Ant. 29. C.P.L. no. 17. Pack² no. 2937. C.L.A., Suppl., 1708.

Lent by the Egypt Exploration Society

22. Fragment of Aeneid XII (762–5, ? 786–790).   4th cent. A.D.

This tiny scrap, the top right-hand corner of a parchment leaf, is all that remains from what must have been a handsome codex in rustic capitals, earlier and somewhat larger than the 'Mediceus' (see no. 28). E. A. Lowe compares the script to that of the 'Vaticanus' (Vat. lat. 3225).

Later history: excavated at Antinoë in 1913–14. Now kept at the Ashmolean Museum.

Bibl.: P. Ant. 30. C.P.L. no. 15. Pack² no. 2952. C.L.A., Suppl., 1709.   Side shown: recto.

Lent by the Egypt Exploration Society

23. Opera.   First half of the 9th cent.

Successive generations of readers have left heavy annotations in this manuscript, especially in Aeneid VI. The pages exhibited (fols. 168ᵛ–169ʳ, Aeneid IX. 264–321, see pl. II) contain glosses by two main hands. The first, working in the 9th cent., added glosses in a mixture of Caroline minuscule and Tironian notes, the ancient system of shorthand which was practised in the Carolingian schools. The second hand, 11th-cent., added long glosses from Servius' commentary, in Aeneid VIII – XII.

The script of the main text has been attributed by Prof. B. Bischoff to the abbey of St.-Germain-des-Prés in Paris. Spaces, left blank at the ends of quires and coinciding with changes of hands (e.g. fols. 110ᵛ/111ʳ), show that the exemplar was divided up for copying among the various members of the scriptorium.

Later history: Jacques Mentel (1597–1671), the Parisian physician, lent the manuscript to Nicholas Heinsius, who did not return it. Heinsius' sale → Edward Bernard.

Bibl.: S.C. 8851. Ellis III, pl. 3 (fol. 103ʳ). Pächt & Alexander, i. 415. R.A.B. Mynors, ed., O.C.T. 1969, p. ix (siglum f).

<u>MS. Auct. F. 2.8</u>   PLATE II

24. <u>Opera</u>, with SERVIUS, etc.   10th cent., perhaps early 11th.

The nucleus of this German manuscript is a copy of Vergil's text. Servius' commentary was written in separate quires in a different style of script, perhaps somewhat later, and bound in after the <u>Georgics</u> and after the <u>Aeneid</u>. Further glosses were added at the same time: interlinear and marginal glosses in the original text; a set of glosses on all three major works of Vergil, written out as a continuous text and preceded by a Life of the poet (pp. 83. I – 102. II, following Servius' commentary on the <u>Georgics</u>); and a miscellaneous section headed 'incipiunt uaria glosemata' (pp. 102. II – 104. II). A few of these glosses could derive ultimately from ancient, non-Servian commentaries on Vergil. Others are in Old High German, and there are even a few in Old English from the 8th-cent. 'Épinal-Erfurt' glossary.

<u>History</u>: 'Qui me scribebat   Tibericus nomen habebat' (this inscription appears on p. 416 at the end of one of the added sections of Servius, but the script, though contemporary, is not identical to any of the main hands). Bernhard Rottendorph of Münster → Nicholas Heinsius → Edward Bernard.

<u>Bibl</u>.: S.C. 8856. J.J.H. Savage, 'The manuscripts of Servius's Commentary on Virgil', Harvard Studies in Classical Philology, 45 (1934), 185-7. R. Bergmann, Verzeichnis der althochdeutschen und altsächsischen Glossenhandschriften (Arbeiten zur Frühmittelalterforschung 6), Berlin & New York 1973, pp. 83-4 no. 721 (gives further refs.). J.D. Pheifer, Old English glosses in the Épinal-Erfurt glossary, Oxford 1974, xl.

<u>MS. Auct. F. 1.16</u>

25. <u>Opera</u>.   Middle of the 12th cent.

Written probably in England in the tall narrow format often used for verse manuscripts. This book bears the inscription 'Liber Magistri Aluredi' (fol. iii^v) in red capitals similar to and contemporary with those in the main text, and an erased monastic ex-libris, 13th-cent. (?), which N. R. Ker has shown to be almost certainly of Cirencester. Master Alfred's identity has not been established, but a possible candidate is the man who attested writs of Henry II, including one for Cirencester abbey of c. 1155.

The manuscript came later into the possession of Henry Penwortham (d. 1438), registrar and treasurer of archbishop Chichele; it is the sole identifiable survivor of the books which Penwortham bequeathed to his master for the latter's new foundation, All Souls College. The present binding, of stamped leather, is said by G. Pollard to have been made at 'Oxford, perhaps by John More, 1465/72'.

Bibl.: Coxe, College MSS. On Master Alfred, see N. R. Ker, 'Sir John Prise', The Library, 5th Ser, 10 (1955), 17, and for the

potential candidate, C. D. Ross, ed., The cartulary of Cirencester Abbey, I, London 1964, p. 54 no. 67. For the binding see

G. Pollard, 'The names of some English fifteenth-century binders', The Library, 5th Ser., 25 (1970), pl. IV (before p. 201).

All Souls College, MS. 82

26-28. POMPONIO LETO AND VERGIL

The work on Vergil of Pomponio Leto (1428-98), founder of the Roman Academy, has been known since his own day from a pirated edition of his glosses which was published by Daniele Gaitano at Brescia in 1487 (Appendix Vergiliana, Bucolics and Georgics. Hain 9836) and 1490 (?) (Aeneid. Hain 9835), in which the author is called 'Pomponius grammaticus eruditissimus', 'doctissimus vir', or 'Pomponius Sabinus'. This careless edition, repudiated by Pomponio himself, was revised by Giovanni Oporino for a new edition printed at Basel in 1544. The material was subsequently incorporated in the glosses to the 1561 Basel edition of Vergil (the Bodleian possesses the reprint of 1586).

Pomponio never published an official version of his glosses. Zabughin's claim that glosses in two Vatican manuscripts of Vergil are partly in Pomponio's hand has now been disproved, although it is true that the glosses in one of them, Vat. lat. 3255, derive from his lectures. The Bodleian possesses a copy of the Aeneid with Pomponio's original glosses, unmistakably autograph but not previously identified as such (no. 26). By a strange chance, the library had also acquired from a different source a fair copy of Pomponio's commentary on the whole Vergilian corpus, which he had reworked into continuous form, perhaps for publication (no. 27). It is therefore possible to compare two stages in the development of Pomponio's commentary. His first set of glosses (no. 26), written into his text over a period of years, was clearly intended for teaching. The second stage, the continuous commentary of no. 27, often follows the earlier notes word for word, but many items are dropped (textual points, interpretations of difficult words, grammatical notes and other short glosses), and other notes are expanded or completely rewritten.

A comparison of the continuous commentary (no. 27) with the Basel reprint of 1586 shows that no. 27 cannot possibly have been the source of Gaitano's printed edition. Gaitano followed Pomponio's first set of glosses (no. 26) very closely, and included the interlinear interpretations of words or phrases, though he sometimes misunderstood the intended order of the glosses. But certain differences, both additions and omissions, suggest that no. 26 was not his direct source either. Both the edition and no. 27 omit most of the Greek found in no. 26.

Bibl.: for Pomponio's work on Vergil, see especially V. Zabughin, Giulio Pomponio Leto, II, Grottaferrata 1910, 61–111, and the article cited below under no. 27. For his accepted autographs, see G. Muzzioli, 'Due nuovi codici autografi di Pomponio Leto...', Italia medioevale e umanistica, 2(1959), 337–352, with plates.

26. Aeneid, glossed by POMPONIO LETO.   Last third of the 15th cent.

The original text was written on paper around 1470 in a humanistic cursive hand by a scribe from Pomponio's circle; he occasionally used the uncial g much favoured by Pomponio and his friends. The watermarks are a hunting-horn (not in Briquet but nearest to his 7686) and scissors (not in Briquet but to be compared with his 3670 and 3675).

The manuscript was worked on in two stages:

1. The originally very corrupt text was corrected. Up to about fol. 30ᵛ the corrections
are by three or more hands, probably pupils of Pomponio; from there on they are
mostly by Pomponio himself, and he also went over the earlier corrections. Pomponio
added a marginal index of names and subjects.

One of the sources for both groups of corrections was the 5th-cent. manuscript
of Vergil now known as the 'Codex Mediceus' or M (now Florence, Laur., Plut. 39,1,
see no. 28). M had belonged to the monastery of Bobbio, and was still there in
1461; it was probably brought to Rome by Gregorio da Crema, formerly abbot of
Bobbio, when he became abbot of San Paolo fuori le mura in 1467. Pomponio
could not have had access to M before the spring of 1469, when he and the other
members of the Academy were released from prison by Pope Paul II, but he must
have had it in his hands by 1471; in that year, Giovanandrea Bussi brought
out his second edition of Vergil (Copinger 6000), and said in his preface that
for a few passages Pomponio had allowed him to consult an ancient manuscript,
generally assumed to have been M.

Most of the corrections from M were entered by Pomponio in no. 26 without
comment. Some can be identified because the readings are unique to M; for others,
chiefly spellings of proper names, he noted that he found the readings 'in antiquo'
or 'in codice antiquo', e.g. fol. 73aʳ, on Aen. VI. 781: 'Semper in antiquo incluta
per u' (pl. III). These readings (on fols. 40ᵛ, 48ᵛ, 55ʳ, 73aʳ, 77ᵛ, 82ʳ, 92ᵛ, 94ʳ, 102ʳ,
106ᵛ, 121ᵛ, 127ᵛ, 151ᵛ, 156ᵛ) are all those of M, with one exception (fol. 94ʳ, possibly
due to a slip of memory by Pomponio). One or two of the 'in antiquo' references
(fols. 94ʳ, 156ᵛ) may have been added at a later stage, but most must be early,
and several (e.g. fol. 73aʳ) are written in a large hand in the same reddish-brown
ink which Pomponio used for many corrections and for his marginal index. It
is surprising that none of these notes referring to the 'codex antiquus' were
reproduced either in Pomponio's reworked commentary (no. 27) or in Gaitano's

edition, although both include other textual comments.

On fol. 104ᵛ Pomponio cites, without mentioning his source, a complete version of two scholia (written by him as one) found in M, fol. 163ᵛ (on <u>Aen.</u> IX. 279 and 281). These have since been cropped in M. Pomponio's original copy of these scholia, in no. 26, is more accurate than would appear from Gaitano's edition (Basel reprint of 1586, col. 1401), or from no. 27 (fol. 311ʳ⁻ᵛ). In no. 27 alone, he attributes them to 'Apromianus'. However, some of the glosses attributed by Pomponio to Apromianus in both nos. 26 and 27 were not derived from M.

M, fol. 163ᵛ (detail).

no. 26, fol. 104ᵛ (detail).

no. 27, fol. 311ʳ (detail).

Basel reprint of 1586, col. 1401 (detail).

no. 27, fol. 311ᵛ (top line).

2.   Later, perhaps for use in lectures, Pomponio added copious glosses, mainly historical and geographical, but including grammatical and textual comments. He probably did this work over a period after 1473, since he once (fol. 26ᵛ) cites his own commentary on

the Georgics, in which he used material gained from his travels in Russia and Eastern Europe in 1472-3. The work was certainly well under way before 1478, for in a gloss added at a late stage, on Aen. VII. 83 'Albunea' (fol. 76ᵛ), he says 'Domitius meus ait locum esse cum pestilenti hiatu unde nomen deductum pro fetore'. This is the only reference to a contemporary among these glosses, and must mean Pomponio's friend Domizio Calderini, who died in the summer of 1478. Domizio's only known work on the Aeneid consists of unpublished excerpts from a commentary on Aeneid VI in Munich, Clm 807, fols. 121ʳ-139ᵛ. The likelihood is that Pomponio had this comment from Domizio's own mouth. It is included in his reworked commentary (no. 27, fols. 280ᵛ-281ʳ) as by 'Domitius noster'. In the 1586 reprint of Gaitano's edition (col.1149) it is unattributed.

Later history: bought as lot 306 in Sotheby's sale 20-21 June 1860, of books and manuscripts 'formerly in the archives of two princely Roman families'. It then had its original binding, claimed, probably over-optimistically, to have been made for Lorenzo de' Medici. However, as the sale catalogue said, the manuscript 'shows every sign of having been the property of no mean scholar'.

Bibl.: S.C. 28750. For the facsimile of M, see no. 28. For M's later history see also G. Mercati, De fatis bibliothecae monasterii S. Columbani Bobiensis..., Prolegomena to M. Tulli Ciceronis De Re Publica e codice rescripto Vat. lat. 5757 phototypice expressi (Codices e Vaticanis selecti, 23), Vatican City 1934, 7+, reaffirmed in Opere minori IV (Studi e Testi 79), Vatican City 1937, 525-6. For a summary of Calderini's life and works, with bibliography, see A. Perosa in Dizionario biografico degli italiani 16 (1973), 597-605.   Page exhibited: fol. 73aʳ, with 'in antiquo' reference.

<u>MS. Add. C. 136</u>   PLATE III

27. POMPONIO LETO, continuous commentary on the complete works of Vergil.   Last third of the 15th cent.

The commentary bears no attribution to Pomponio, but the author was identified by Coxe as 'Julius Pomponius Sabinus' on the basis of the Basel reprint of 1586. The manuscript is not autograph, as Zabughin thought, but a fair copy by a scribe. However, there is at least one added note in Pomponio's hand (fol. 142ᵛ). It was written by a scribe from Pomponio's circle who sometimes used his uncial g . This scribe may also have copied the first part of the manuscript of Domizio Calderini's commentary on Martial which he presented to Lorenzo de' Medici in 1473 (Florence, Laur., Plut. 53,33). The paper has watermarks of a cardinal's hat (nearest to Briquet 3371) and of a hunting-horn, apparently the same as that found in no. 26. But the hand of no. 27 and the text hand of no. 26 do not belong to the same scribe.

The manuscript appears to have been carelessly copied, perhaps from another fair copy. It contains glosses on all the works of Vergil and includes Pomponio's Life of Vergil, which draws heavily on Ps.-Probus. In the glosses on the Appendix Vergiliana there are references to Pomponio's own commentaries on Livy, Tacitus and Silius Italicus.

Later history: fol. iʳ, two ex-libris apparently of the 16th cent.: 'Est Io. Rutini et amicorum' and 'Benedicti Varicensii'
(perhaps identifiable as Benedetto Varchi, 1503–65, the Florentine historian).

Bibl.: Coxe, Canonici MSS., cols. 133-4. V. Zabughin, 'L'autografo delle chiose vergiliane di Pomponio Leto…', L'Arcadia
3 (1918), 135-151. Laur., Plut. 53,33 was reproduced by J. Dunston in Italia medioevale e umanistica 11 (1968),
pls. III - V.

Page exhibited: fol. 268ᵛ (for omission of Greek, compare line 12 here with no. 26, fol. 72ᵛ bottom margin, exhibited).

MS. Canon. Class. Lat. 54

28. VERGIL, Opera : 'Codex Mediceus' (facsimile).   5th cent.

This parchment codex was written in rustic capitals, probably at Rome, where it was corrected and punctuated by Turcius Rufius Apronianus Asterius, consul in A.D. 494. His subscription on fol. 8ʳ is written in a minute script in the blank spaces left between the lines of the closing title of the Eclogues.

This modern facsimile is one of the most life-like ever produced of a manuscript.

Complete facsimile, with introduction by E. Rostagno, 'Notizie intorno al 'Virgilio Mediceo', Rome 1931. C.L.A., III, no. **296.

<u>Page exhibited</u>: fol. 129ʳ, 4th line from bottom, <u>Aen</u>. VI. 781, the source for Pomponio's 'in antiquo' reference exhibited in no. 26, fol. 73aʳ.

<u>Florence, Biblioteca Medicea Laurenziana, Plut. 39, 1</u> (facsimile)

29. P. B. SHELLEY, Translation of <u>Ecl</u>. X. 1–30.   1819 or before

This fragmentary translation survives in two drafts in Shelley's handwriting on successive pages of a notebook (fols. 59ʳ⁻ᵛ and 60ʳ⁻ᵛ). Fol. 60ᵛ, exhibited, shows the end of the second draft:

> 'The meadows with fresh streams, the bees with thyme
>
> The goats with the green leaves of budding spring
>
> Are saturated not — nor Love with tears.'

These lines are a translation of <u>Eclogues</u> X. 28–30:

> '... Amor non talia curat,
>
> nec lacrimis crudelis Amor nec gramina riuis
>
> nec cytiso saturantur apes nec fronde capellae.'

The facing page, fol. 61ʳ, shows a tiny scrap relating to <u>Georgics</u> IV. 317–321 (Aristaeus). The blank spaces at the bottoms of both pages were used later by Shelley to hold the end of his translation of Euripides' <u>Cyclops</u> (Gk. original lines 676–709, tr. lines 685–718), which Shelley was writing in 1819 when he 'could do absolutely nothing else'; this may be the first draft.

<u>History</u>: from the donation made by Jane Lady Shelley, the poet's daughter-in-law, in 1893–4.

<u>Bibl</u>.: S.C. 31555. C. D. Locock, <u>An Examination of the Shelley manuscripts in the Bodleian Library</u>, Oxford 1903, 40–75, esp. 47–50.

MS. Shelley e. 4

Ancient Books
30-34. From roll to codex

The transition from roll to codex has been described as 'the most momentous development in the history of the book until the invention of printing' (C.H. Roberts, p. 169). To illustrate what an ancient roll looked like, we show over eight columns of an opened roll (no. 5), and the charred husks of three closed rolls (no. 30). Martial's poems show that the codex was being used for literary texts in his time. However the reading public was very conservative, and although the codex was early adopted for Christian texts, it was only during the course of the 4th cent. that it became the predominant form for all sorts of literature. The earliest Greek codex exhibited is the Callimachus (no. 44) of the 4th cent. Of our Latin exhibits from that century, the Livy (no. 49) is still in roll form, but the Vergils (nos. 21, 22) are from codices. They are small fragments excavated in Egypt; a better idea of the the appearance of an ancient codex can be gained from the 5th-cent. Eusebius (no. 34), which has survived almost intact above ground.

Papyrus was the normal material for books until later antiquity. Three 6th-cent. examples are exhibited (nos. 10, 52, 53). The earliest example of parchment shown is the 4th-cent. scrap of Vergil (no. 22). In the course of the 5th cent., 'the parchment codex tends more and more to supersede its papyrus counterpart, even in Egypt' (C.H. Roberts, p. 203).

Strictly speaking, wooden writing-tablets do not come into our story, since they were not used for books but for smaller items such as documents (nos. 31, 32) and for anything of an impermanent nature (no. 33) – sums, school exercises, or an author's first draft. But it is important to realise that in their arrangement in sets they are the immediate precursors of books in codex form. Our three examples are of the usual type – a flat piece of wood with a central area hollowed out to receive a film of wax, on which writing could be scratched with a metal stylus. The tablets were commonly put in sets of two up to as many as ten leaves, tied together on one side to open as a 'book'; no. 32 is a diptych, a set of two leaves, and no. 33 must have been an inner leaf from a polyptych. In Cicero's time a set of wax tablets could properly be called a codex, but it was only much later that the word came to denote a book.

The page exhibited in our copy of the <u>Notitia Dignitatum</u> (no. 146, fol. 146^v) shows representations (ultimately deriving from a late antique model) of rolls and sets of writing-tablets, the insignia of the 'Magistri scriniorum' of the Occident.

<u>Bibl.</u>: C. H. Roberts, 'The codex', <u>Proceedings of the British Academy</u>, 40 (1954), 169 – 204.

30. Three carbonized papyrus rolls, unopened, from Herculaneum.

Before A.D. 79.

In A.D. 79, Herculaneum was buried in volcanic ash by the eruption of Vesuvius. Excavators discovered there in 1752 a library of papyrus rolls. It must have had some connection with the Epicurean Philodemus (c. 110 – c. 40 / 35 B.C.), for texts relevant to his work are the chief contents of those rolls which have successfully been opened. Other rolls have been completely destroyed in the attempt. A fourth Bodleian roll was opened at Naples in 1883, but little could be read (now Ms. Gr. class. b. 1 (P) / 1 - 12).

<u>Later history</u>: between 1803 and 1806, eighteen unopened rolls and two already unrolled were presented by Ferdinand IV, king of Naples and Sicily, to the Prince of Wales (later George IV), who was financing work on the papyri by the Rev. John Hayter. The Prince gave four of the unopened rolls, and a fragment of a fifth which has since disappeared, to the University of Oxford in 1810, and advised caution in unrolling them. Others are now in the British Library.

Bibl.: S.C. 28048-50 (Herculaneum inventory nos.: burnt rolls 149, 161, 172). Exh. Pap. 1974, nos. 16-18. W. Scott, *Fragmenta Herculanensia*, Oxford 1885, 2-8.

MSS. Gr. class. f. 25-27 (P)

31-33. WRITING TABLETS

31. Fragment of a birth certificate, in Latin.   A.D. 147

In its original state this document must have resembled no. 32, as it does in style of script. The two lines which remain of the wax surface preserve the dating clause:

L. ANNIO LARGO C. PRASTINA MESSALINO COS.

IIII K(AL). SEPTEMBRES ANNO X̄ IMP. CAESARIS

These are the names of the consuls for A.D. 147, the tenth year of the reign of Antoninus Pius. As in no. 32, a copy for reference was written in ink directly onto the wooden surface of the side without wax, but sideways not lengthways, so that there survive the beginnings of fourteen lines from which the nature of the document can be determined.   Later history: from Egypt. Bought from B.P. Grenfell in 1896.

Bibl.: S.C. 32409. C.P.L. no. 155. First published, with facsimile, by S. de Ricci (using E.W.B. Nicholson's transcript) in *Proceedings of the Society of Biblical Archaeology*, 26 (1904), 195-6 and pl. IV, and again by R. Cagnat, 'Extraits de naissance égyptiens', *Journal des Savants* 1927, 198-9 no. 8. F. Schulz, 'Roman registers of births and birth certificates', *Journal of Roman Studies*, 32 (1942), 79 no. 8.

Ms. Lat. class. e. 16 (P)

32. Appointment of a guardian.   A.D. 198

This diptych contains the appointment of a guardian for a woman by the prefect of Egypt. The main body of the text inscribed on the wax is in Latin, followed by a subscription written in Greek by an amanuensis on behalf of the woman, who was illiterate. On the outside there are copies of these sections and a list of the names of seven witnesses, all written in ink directly on the wood. The diptych was originally tied shut and sealed with the seals of the witnesses to prevent tampering with the inner text, the authenticated version, while the exterior text remained available for consultation. The Latin script is capital cursive.

The state of preservation of this 2nd-cent. document is remarkable.

Later history: acquired in Cairo by A.H.Sayce shortly before he gave it in 1919.

Bibl.: B.P.Grenfell, 'A Latin-Greek diptych of A.D.198', B.Q.R. 2(1919), 258-262. C.P.L. no. 202. Exh. Pap. 1974, no.31.

MSS. Lat. class. f. 9 - 10 (P) (formerly MSS. Lat. inscr. 10-11).

33. Leaf from a polyptych.   Date uncertain

Unlike nos. 31 and 32, this tablet has wax on both sides, and was probably therefore an inner leaf from a set of several tablets. The small surfaces left raised in the middle of each side were to prevent the writing on the wax being smudged when the polyptych was closed. Holes for the thongs in three groups of two are visible down one side. The wax is now badly perished, but some marks are still visible, possibly accounts or sums.

Later history : from Egypt. Given with a number of Coptic pieces by A.C. Headlam in 1895.

MS. Gr. class. f. 124 (P) (formerly MS. Copt. Inscr. 10 and MS. Gr. Inscr. 13)

34. EUSEBIUS - Jerome, Chronicle, etc.   Middle of the 5th cent. (after A.D. 435 or 442)

Written in uncials, with contemporary corrections and marginal index in sloping bd-uncials. The book has all the appearance of a working copy. It exhibits the squarish format of an ancient codex also to be seen in the facsimile of the 'Mediceus' of Vergil. The parchment is of 'the fine Italian type, in parts very thin, but with many blemishes' (E. A. Lowe).

Our manuscript was not the only ancient copy of the text to survive into the Middle Ages: there still exist fragments of another 5th-cent. copy which had reached Fleury by the 9th cent. (C.L.A., V no. 563). The medieval home of the Bodleian manuscript is unknown. Its few descendants appear to be Italian, but in the first half of the 15th cent. its first four quires were replaced by leaves (fols. 1–32) of which the script and decoration suggest an origin in the south of France.

Later history: extensive annotations passim (including fols. 1–32) by a 15th-cent. cursive hand. Jean du Tillet, bishop of Meaux (d. 1570). Clermont → Meerman. The manuscript did not become known to the learned world until the visit to the Bodleian of Theodor Mommsen c. 1888. Its 'discovery' by a foreign scholar caused considerable indignation in Oxford, and was one of the contributory factors which led to the cataloguing of the entire Bodleian collections in the Summary Catalogue (see R.W. Hunt in S.C., vol. I, pp. lix–lx, and E.W.B. Nicholson in Journal of Philology, 20 (1892), 134).

Bibl.: S.C. 20632. Pächt & Alexander, i. 684 (fols. 1–32). Complete facsimile ed. J.K. Fotheringham, The Bodleian manuscript of the chronicle of Eusebius, Oxford 1905. C.L.A. II, 2nd ed., no. 233a.

Pages exhibited: fols. 86ᵛ–87ʳ (Olympiads LXXXVI – XCIII, 433–405 B.C.).

MS. Auct. T. 2. 26, fols. 33–145

35–44. Greek Literary Papyri

In a sense the papyri dug up in modern times are irrelevant to the history of the transmission of ancient texts, since by their very nature, being found below rather than above ground, they represent dead traditions. However they are important not only because they have enlarged our stock of ancient literature (e.g. nos. 38, 39, 42) but because they often give us improvements to the texts of authors already known (e.g. no. 35). No. 43 allowed us to redate an ancient author by a couple of centuries. They also provoke reflections on the reading habits of the educated public in Greco-Roman Egypt. The importance of Oxyrhynchus as a site for literary finds is demonstrated by the fact that it is the source of eight of the ten items in this section.

Bibl.: for statistics about the papyri of the main authors, see W. H. Willis in Greek, Roman and Byzantine Studies, 9 (1968), 205-41.

35. Fragment of PLATO, Laches.   Early 3rd cent. B.C.

An important and very early papyrus of Plato, extracted from cartonnage (see no. 1). This copy of the text exhibits several variant readings which are now regarded as improvements to the text as known from the medieval tradition.

History: from Gurob. Given by Jesse Haworth (see no. 3) in 1895.   Bibl.: P. Petrie II 50. Pack² no. 1409. Exh. Pap. 1974, no. 1.

MS. Gr. class. d. 22 (P) (and d. 23 (P), not shown)

36. Fragment of an unidentified tragedy.   1st cent. A.D.

From the vocabulary used in this fragment it has been inferred that the text is probably post-Euripidean. So little of 4th-cent. tragedy survives that further conjecture about the author is not profitable.   History: 'bought in Cairo. From Eshmunein' (Hermopolis). Given by Mrs. A. S. Hunt, 1934.

Bibl.: E. Lobel in Greek poetry and life. Essays presented to Gilbert Murray ... Oxford 1936, 295-8, with pl. Pack² no. 1710. Exh. Pap. 1974, no. 13.

MS. Gr. class. f. 113 (P)

37. Fragments of CALLIMACHUS, Aitia.   1st cent. A.D.

The papyri have probably added more to our knowledge of Callimachus than of any other author apart from Menander. This specimen is part of a fine copy of one of Callimachus' most important and influential works. Accents and punctuation have been added by a second hand; since the poem makes considerable demands on the reader, these aids will have been welcome.   Bibl.: P. Oxy. 1362 (given in 1923). Pack² no. 216. Exh. Pap. 1974, no. 14.

MS. Gr. class. c. 77 (P)

38. Fragments of ALCAEUS.   2nd cent. A.D.

The early lyric poets Alcaeus and Sappho (no. 39) have also become a good deal better known thanks to discoveries among the papyri. Since they wrote in the Aeolic dialect, which was no longer spoken in the Roman imperial age, their texts needed a certain amount of explanation, and this example has marginal comments in a cursive hand. Accents and the makron sign to designate some long vowels have also been added.

Bibl.: P.Oxy. 1234 + 1360 + 2166(c)(given in 1923). Pack² no.59. Exh. Pap. 1974, no. 22.

MS. Gr. class. a. 16 (P)/1 (the first of three frames)

39. Fragments of SAPPHO, Bk. I.   2nd cent. A.D.

These fragments are from the end of Bk. I of Sappho's lyrics, and a note under the title in the lower right-hand fragment in the frame indicates that the book consisted of 1320 verses. Such notes, described as stichometric, were probably not intended to serve the same purpose as line numbers in a modern printed text but to allow calculation of the payment due to a professional scribe.

Bibl.: P.Oxy. 1231 + 2166(a)(given in 1923). Pack² no. 1445. Exh. Pap. 1974, no. 23.

MS. Gr. class. c. 76 (P)/2 (the second of two frames)

40. Fragments of HERODOTUS, Bk. II.   Late 2nd cent. A.D.

The note in smaller script in the top right-hand corner records a variant reading from other copies. Notes of this kind are not unknown in other papyri. They indicate the concern of intelligent readers in antiquity to establish the text in passages where it seemed dubious.

Bibl.: P.Oxy. 1092 (given in 1921). Pack² no. 473. Exh. Pap. 1974, no. 27. For a general discussion of such notes, see E.G. Turner, 'Scribes and scholars of Oxyrhynchus', Mitteilungen aus der Papyrussammlung der Österreichischen Nationalbibliothek, N.S.5(1956),141-6, with plates.   MS. Gr. class. d. 114 (P)

41. Fragment of the Acta Maximi.   2nd cent. A.D.

This exhibit belongs to an unsavoury class of ancient pamphlets known as the Acts of the Pagan Martyrs: they are documents of racial hatred, produced in Alexandria and designed to inflame the feelings of the Hellenised population against the Roman government.

Bibl.: P.Oxy. 471 (given in 1906). Pack² no. 2225. Exh.Pap. 1974, no. 29.   MS. Gr. class. a. 10 (P)

42. Fragment of LYSIAS. Late 2nd or early 3rd cent. A.D.

The surviving fragments from this beautiful roll of Lysias' speeches include the end of his oration Against Hippotherses, otherwise lost, in which Lysias defended his own conduct during the brief period in 404 B.C. when democracy in Athens was replaced by the Oligarchy of the Thirty. The closing title is visible in the middle of the third column of the fragment exhibited.

Bibl.: P.Oxy. 1606 (given in 1923). Pack² no. 1293. Exh.Pap. 1974, no. 37. Discussed by K.J.Dover, Lysias and the Corpus

Lysiacum, Berkeley 1968, 28, 34, 40-41.

MS. Gr. class. b. 19 (P)/1 (the first of three frames)

43. ACHILLES TATIUS, Clitophon and Leucippe. Late 3rd or early 4th cent. A.D.?

This papyrus demonstrates that the novelist Achilles Tatius cannot be dated to the 5th or 6th cent. A.D. as he used to be. Another, still earlier fragment, perhaps belonging to the 2nd cent., has been found more recently (P. Mil. Vogl. 124).

Bibl.: P.Oxy. 1250 (given in 1914). Pack² no. 2. Exh.Pap. 1974, no. 45.

MS. Gr. class. d. 97 (P)

44. Fragments of CALLIMACHUS, Aitia & Iambi. 4th cent. A.D.

The Bodleian possesses seven leaves of this papyrus codex; the first is shown. The ink, being metallic instead of based on carbon, has faded, but can be read rather better under ultra-violet light. These fragments were the first continuous passages from the texts to be published (in 1910). Bibl.: P.Oxy. 1011 (given in 1921). Pack² no. 215. Exh.Pap. 1974, no. 48.

MS. Gr. class. c. 72 (P)/1

45-53. Latin Papyri

The number of Latin manuscripts recovered by excavation is insignificant compared with the Greek, and there is no agreement among scholars as to what was the normal script of Latin books. Jean Mallon, who has been instrumental in focussing attention on the problem, believes that the normal script was what he calls the 'écriture commune', that is, scripts more or less cursive, whereas the codices in rustic capitals from the 4th and 5th centuries which have survived above ground, such as the 'Mediceus' of Vergil (see no. 28), were luxury products and do not fairly represent the norm.

It cannot be denied that 'écriture commune' was used for all purposes, including books. Our two wax-tablets of the 2nd cent. A.D. (nos. 31 and 32) are documents written in capital cursive script, and the Egypt Exploration Society has kindly lent us an even earlier specimen, a private letter from the end of the 1st cent. B.C. (no. 45). Nos. 46-8 show the script used in books of the 2nd and 3rd centuries A.D. Nevertheless, it was not the only all-purpose script, and it is not certain that it was the norm. A more likely candidate in the early Empire is rustic capital script. Our one small fragment is later, from a 4th-cent. Vergil (no. 22). But G. P. Nicolaj has recently published photographs of more Latin papyri from Herculaneum (i.e. before A.D. 79) in a variety of rustic capital scripts. The Romans had high standards of lettering, and rustic capital script was a favourite form. One has only to go around Pompeii or Ostia and look at the inscriptions of the butcher, the baker and the candlestick-maker to see this.

The fine 5th-cent. uncial script of our Eusebius (no. 34) is familiar to us from other extant manuscripts, but the finds of Latin papyri have brought to light examples of scripts hardly known to us previously, or have extended our knowledge of the range of application possible for scripts already represented in the manuscripts.

The main text of the Vergil (no. 21), and the Livy (no. 49), both of the 4th cent., are written in a form named by E. A. Lowe 'bd-uncial', which used to be best known to us as a script for marginalia (as in no. 34) and for chapter-headings. An early half-uncial form, 4th-cent., appears in the Sallust (no. 50) and in the subsidiary material of no. 21. Examples of the later type of uncial with characteristic letters B and R, hitherto represented mainly by the 6th-cent. Florentine Pandects (C.L.A. III, no. 295), have now emerged in copies of Homer (P.S.I. I 10, see Cavallo & Manfredi cited below) and Juvenal (no. 51). No. 52 shows this script in a legal work which can be closely dated, and the Graeco-Latin legal fragment (no. 53) illustrates its suitability for both languages. Our examples show that this script could be used for literary as well as legal texts, and strengthen the possibility that it was being written in Egypt.

The problem of the place where the Latin papyri found in Egypt were written is one which needs reconsideration. If they show any distinction, they tend to be regarded as importations. This is only assumed to hold for Greek papyri in very exceptional circumstances. But in view of 'the widespread Latinization of Egypt after Diocletian's reforms and the efflorescence of Roman studies there' (G. M. Browne), it is surely as likely that most of the Latin fragments discovered there were written in Egypt itself.

Bibl.: J. Mallon, Paléographie romaine (Scripturae monumenta et studia, 3), Madrid 1952. G. P. Nicolaj in Miscellanea in memoria di Giorgio Cencetti, Turin 1973, pls. II–IV. G. Cavallo & M. Manfredi in Proceedings of the XIV International Congress of Papyrologists 1974 = Graeco-Roman Memoirs, 61 (1975), 47-58, pl. XII. G. M. Browne, ibid., 31.

45. Letter of Syneros to his friend Chius.   End of the 1st cent. B.C.(?)

A well-preserved private letter, perhaps referring to some financial transaction and probably dating from the reign of Augustus. Found at Oxyrhynchus. Both the writer and the addressee have Greek names, but the letter is written in colloquial Latin. The script is the old capital cursive, and the words are separated by points.

Bibl.: Oxyrhynchus Parcel 34. Box 4B/76L(2-3), shortly to be published as P.Oxy.3208. V. Brown, 'A Latin letter from Oxyrhynchus', *University of London. Institute of Classical Studies. Bulletin*, 17(1970), 136-143, pl. IV.

<u>Lent by the Egypt Exploration Society</u>

46. Latin fragment on the institutions of Servius Tullius.   2nd cent. A.D.

Fragment, found at Oxyrhynchus, from a papyrus roll. F.M. Heichelheim, citing a parallel passage in Dionysius of Halicarnassus, IV.xv,1, suggests that this is a fragment of Cato the Censor's lost <u>Origines</u>, Bk.I. The script is 'a regulated cursive of the early Roman type, probably used for inexpensive books' (E.A.Lowe).

Bibl.: P.Oxy. 2088 (now kept at the Ashmolean Museum). C.P.L. no.41. Pack² no. 2999. <u>C.L.A.</u>, Suppl., no.1714. Text discussed by F.M. Heichelheim in <u>Aegyptus</u>, 37(1957), 250-258.

<u>Lent by the Egypt Exploration Society</u>

47. Fragment of GAIUS, <u>Institutiones</u> (IV.57; 68-72ᵇ).   2nd (end) or 3rd cent. A.D.

This fragment of a papyrus roll, found at Oxyrhynchus, is two centuries earlier than the Verona palimpsest (<u>C.L.A.</u> IV, no. 488), and cannot be much more than a century later than the author's own copy. Lowe describes the script as a 'regular, restrained cursive' of the early Roman type 'in a hand conscious of writing a book', and compares it with no. 46. Bibl.: P.Oxy. 2103 (now kept at the Ashmolean Museum). C.P.L. no.77. Pack² no. 2954. C.L.A., Suppl., no.1716.

<u>Lent by the Egypt Exploration Society</u>

48. Fragment on jurisprudence.   3rd cent. A.D.

From a papyrus roll; found at Batn-Harît in the Fayum. The script is a calligraphic capital cursive of the early Roman type. Around the middle of the 3rd cent., the verso was used for writing in Greek cursive.

The text contains an edict of Trajan 'de testamento militis', preserved in <u>Dig</u>. XXIX.I,I through Ulpian, <u>Ad edictum</u>, Bk. XLV. But the papyrus includes more than is found there.   <u>Bibl</u>.: P.Fay. 10 (given by the Egypt Exploration Fund in 1900). <u>C.P.L.</u> no. 71. Pack² no. 2991. <u>C.L.A.</u>

II, 2nd ed., no. 249. See also R. Marichal in <u>Scriptorium</u>, 9 (1955), 128. Another fragment is preserved at Berlin,

Aegyptisches Museum, P. 11533, see <u>C.L.A.</u>, Suppl., p. 2.

<u>MS. Lat. class. g. 5</u> (P)

49. Fragment of LIVY, Bk. I (v, 7–vi, 1).   4th cent. A.D.

This fragment, written in 'bd-uncial', is from a papyrus roll. Found at Oxyrhynchus. Although potentially important as predating the copy made for Symmachus (see no. 88), the text provides nothing unexpected.

<u>Bibl</u>.: P.Oxy. 1379 (given in 1923). <u>C.P.L.</u> no. 35. Pack² no. 2926. <u>C.L.A.</u> II, 2nd ed., no. 247. Exh. Pap. 1974, no. 44. R.M.Ogilvie,

ed., Bks. I–V, <u>O.C.T.</u> 1974, vi.   <u>MS. Lat. class. f. 5</u> (P)

50. Fragment of SALLUST, <u>Catilina</u> (vi, 2–7).   5th cent. A.D.

Part of a leaf of a papyrus codex found at Oxyrhynchus. 'Script shows an early stage of half-uncial, with letters varying greatly in size and yet producing a calligraphic effect' (E. A. Lowe).

The text contains a large number of errors. This is often the case when the texts of newly-exhumed papyri can be compared with the living tradition of the medieval manuscripts. The fragment happens to coincide with passages quoted by St. Augustine, and includes a clause found elsewhere only in St. Augustine's quotation.

<u>Bibl</u>.: P.Oxy. 884 (given in 1914). <u>C.P.L.</u> no. 32. Pack² no. 2931. <u>C.L.A.</u>, II, 2nd ed., no. 246. A. Ernout, ed., Budé 1958, 42–3.

<u>MS. Lat. class. e. 20</u> (P)

51. Fragment of JUVENAL (VII. 149–198).   End of the 5th or early 6th cent.

Part of a single leaf from a parchment codex, written in uncials of the type found in the Florentine Pandects. The discovery of this fragment at Antinoë provided important new evidence for the reading of Latin poetry in Egypt at this date, although the number of Latin fragments other than Vergil among the finds can still be counted on the fingers of one hand. The text is sound, and substantially the same as that represented by the medieval manuscripts. The marginal and interlinear notes in Greek and Latin, by more than one 6th-cent. hand, are independent of the ancient scholia which descended to the medieval manuscripts; although of poor quality, their bookish, grammatical character suggests Alexandria as their source. The text is also embellished with marks of quantity, accent-marks, and what appear to be critical signs.

Bibl.: P. Ant., S.N. (now kept at the Ashmolean Museum). C.H. Roberts in Journal of Egyptian Archaeology, 21 (1935), 199–209, pls. XXIV–XXV. C.P.L. no. 37. Pack² no. 2925. C.L.A., Suppl., no. 1710.

Side shown: verso.   Lent by the Egypt Exploration Society

52. Fragment of an index to the first edition of Justinian's Codex.
A.D. 529–534

Justinian's Codex as we know it is the second edition, produced in A.D. 534 and embodying many new decisions and constitutions made since the original edition of A.D. 529. This mutilated leaf discovered at Oxyrhynchus is from a papyrus codex which contained an index of rubrics and inscriptions to the lost first edition. In a comparison with the corresponding titles of the second edition, some important readings are supplied in those titles common to both, and the differences give us an insight into the nature of the revisers' task.

The fragment must have been written before the issue of the second edition, which included a clause prohibiting the use of the earlier version. It is therefore of palaeographical importance as a dated example of its script, the type of uncials used in the Florentine Pandects.   Bibl.: P. Oxy. 1814 (kept at the Ashmolean Museum). C.P.L. no. 101. Pack² 2969.

C.L.A., Suppl., no. 1713.   Lent by the Egypt Exploration Society

53. Fragment on the Law of Dowry, in Latin and Greek.

First half of the 6th cent.

This fragment, found at Antinoë, is the lower corner of a leaf from a large papyrus codex. The text is in a mixture of Greek and Latin words. Large margins were left to accommodate the extensive marginalia, written in smaller script by the scribe of the main text. Uncial script of the Florentine Pandects type.

Bibl.: P. Ant. 152 (now kept at the Ashmolean Museum). C.L.A., Suppl., no. 1711.

Lent by the Egypt Exploration Society

Greek

54-72. Byzantium, c. 850 – c. 1400.

54. ARISTOTLE, Biological works.

Middle of the 9th cent.

Probably the earliest manuscript of these texts. The hand is pure minuscule, with only an occasional uncial λ at line ends. Breathings and accents were used sporadically by the original scribe. There are annotations by Greek hands of the 12th and 13th centuries.

A list of contents has been added on the last page (fol. 183ᵛ) in an English hand of the mid-13th cent., which may be that of Robert Grosseteste, one of the earliest

Englishmen to study Greek. Two titles and a few words of the 13th-cent. Latin translation by William of Moerbeke were added (e.g. on fols. 161ᵛ, shown, and 178ᵛ) in an English humanistic hand possibly identifiable as that of John Farley (d. 1464), fellow of New College and registrar of Oxford University, whose study of Greek is known from other manuscripts.   <u>Later history</u>: given by Henry Parry in 1623.

<u>Bibl.</u>: Coxe, College MSS. Exh. Byz. 1966, no. 37. Wilson, pl. 12. For Farley, see Exh. Duke Humfrey 1970, no. 39.

<u>Page exhibited</u>: fol. 161ᵛ, the beginning of <u>De longitudine et brevitate vitae</u>, with Latin annotations by the 15th-cent. English hand.

Corpus Christi College, MS. 108

55. EUCLID, <u>Elements</u>.   A.D. 888.

Finished in Sept. 888 by Stephanus clericus, and bought by Arethas of Patrae (bishop of Caesarea, 902 – c. 939) for 14 nomismata. The hand of Stephanus is pure minuscule; Arethas added the scholia and some additional matter in small uncials. This is the oldest manuscript of a classical Greek author to bear a date, although the Vienna Dioscorides can be dated fairly precisely (to c. 512).

The manuscript was much used and annotated from the 10th to the 14th centuries.

<u>Bibl.</u>: S.C. 17179. Exh. Byz. 1966, no. 4. Wilson, pl. 13.

<u>Pages exhibited</u>: the end of <u>Elements</u> Bk. XI, with alternative diagrams for proposition 39 (fol. 305ᵛ), and Bk. XII. 1 (fol. 306ʳ).

MS. D'Orville 301   BACK COVER (fol. 305ᵛ)

56. 'The Clarke Plato'.   A.D. 895.

PLATO, Tetralogies 1–6 (i.e. <u>Euthyphro</u>–<u>Meno</u>), with some scholia.

Finished in November 895 by Johannes calligraphus for Arethas, who paid 21 nomismata for the copying and the parchment. Johannes wrote only the text. Scholia were added in uncial by Arethas and at least one other contemporary. There are annotations by many later hands. This is the oldest manuscript of these Tetralogies, and is perhaps the first volume of a 2-volume copy of the whole of Plato, the second volume of which has not been certainly identified.

Later history: acquired by the monastery of St. John on the island of Patmos between the inventory of 1382 and the extracts taken from the main catalogue for Lollino in 1581 or 1582. It was bought from there by E.D. Clarke in 1801. He lent it to Richard Porson, who foliated and indexed it.

Bibl.: S.C. 18400. Exh. Byz. 1966, no. 5. Complete facsimile, ed. T. W. Allen, Leiden 1898. Wilson, pl. 14.

Page shown: fol. 368ᵛ, the end of the Protagoras and beginning of the Gorgias, with scholia by Arethas and others.

MS. E.D. Clarke 39

57. PHOTIUS, Letters.

Probably late 9th cent.

The earliest manuscript of the text. Fol. 194ʳ (top), exhibited, contains letter 150, in which Photius alludes to Aristophanes' Plutus. This disproves the common fallacy that he never read classical poetry.

Bibl.: Coxe, Greek MSS., cols. 383-4. Exh. Byz. 1966, no. 7. B. Laourdas in Ἀθηνᾶ 55 (1951), 125-154, with facs. Wilson, pl. 15.

MS. Barocci 217

58. THEOPHANES, Chronicle.

Probably late 9th cent.

One of the oldest manuscripts of this important chronicle of events from the reign of Diocletian onwards. Fols. 149ᵛ-150ʳ, exhibited, contain part of the account of the Nika riots in Constantinople in 532.

Later history: given by W. Wake (1657-1737), archbishop of Canterbury. Bibl.: Wilson, pl. 17, and in Dumbarton Oaks Papers, 26 (1972), 357-60.

Christ Church, MS. Wake 5

59. Miscellany.

First half of the 10th cent.

Collection of texts, grammatical, lexicographical, poetical, etc., including inter alia the earliest copies of Musaeus, Hero and Leander, the Batrachomyomachia, and probably of the Physiologus. Bibl.: Coxe, Greek MSS., cols. 70-78. Exh. Byz. 1966, no. 9. Wilson, pls. 20-21.

Page exhibited: fol. 358ʳ, beginning of the Batrachomyomachia.

MS. Barocci 50

60. JOHN MALALAS of Antioch, Chronicle.   11th cent.

The chronicle covers the time from the mythological era to the author's own day at the end of the reign of Justinian. It is the first major work known to have been written in colloquial Greek. This is the principal witness to the Greek text (there is a Slavonic version which preserves the text in more complete form).

Bibl.: Coxe, Greek MSS., col. 304. Exh. Byz. 1966, no. 13. Wilson, pl. 34.

Page exhibited: fol. 250ᵛ, the beginning of Bk. 16, on the accession of Anastasius (491–518).   MS. Barocci 182

61. EPICTETUS, Lectures (published by Arrian), etc.   11th cent.

The scholia on Epictetus have been attributed to Arethas. For all its contents, this is the earliest manuscript and the archetype from which all others were copied.

Later history: Saibante.   Bibl.: Coxe, Greek MSS., Misc. 251. Exh. Byz. 1966, no. 12. Wilson, pl. 35.

Pages exhibited: fols. 131ᵛ–132ʳ show the end of Epictetus, Bk. 3, and the chapter-headings and beginning of Bk. 4.

MS. Auct. T. 4. 13

62. EUCLID, Elements.   12th cent.

The interest of this book is that the scribe used Arabic numerals in his marginal entries (see the diagrams in the lower margins of both pages exhibited, fols. 126ᵛ–127ʳ, Elements IX. 7–9; the numerals on plate IV(a) are later additions). On fol. 126ᵛ, he calculates 2^2 2^3 etc. and $3^2 3^3$ etc.; on fol. 127ʳ (plate IV(b)) he calculates $4^2 4^3$ etc. and $8^2 8^3$ etc. up to $8^6 = 262144$. He understands how to use zero in various positions, which at this date is notable (the book used to be dated to the 14th cent., but the script must be earlier). The use of Arabic numerals was not popularised in Byzantium until the second half of the 13th cent., but restricted use of them by professional mathematicians at an earlier date does not seem inconceivable.

Later history: acquired not later than c. 1800.

Bibl.: Coxe, Greek MSS., Misc. 117. S.C. 30325. For the use of Arabic numerals in Byzantium, see N.G. Wilson, An anthology of

Byzantine prose, Berlin 1971, 126 – note, however, that the Arabic numerals in MS. D'Orville 301, fol. 32ᵛ, there referred to, are

in a later hand, not by the scribe or one of his contemporaries.   **MS. Auct. F. 6. 23**

63. XENOPHON, Cyropaedia.   Probably 12th cent.

A finely written book, apparently neglected by editors of the text even though it
is one of the oldest extant copies.   Later history: given by Thomas Cecill in 1618. Bibl.: Coxe, Greek MSS., Misc. 98.

Pages exhibited: fols. 26ᵛ–27ʳ, part of Bk. II with marginalia by the scribe and by another hand, probably later.

MS. Auct. F. 3. 24   PLATE V

64. Miscellany.   13th cent.

This volume, an enormous collection of classical and medieval texts, is the unique
source of some works of Byzantine literature. Fols. 310ᵛ–311ʳ, exhibited, contain the
end of Menander Rhetor and the beginning of declamations of Himerios. The
former, collated recently for the first time, proved to contain a clause of the text not
previously known.   Bibl.: Coxe, Greek MSS., cols. 211–230. Exh. Byz. 1966, no. 27. Wilson, pls. 58–62.

MS. Barocci 131

65. Miscellany.   13th cent.

Another varied collection. Fols. 12ᵛ–13ʳ, exhibited, contain Aristotle's Rhetoric,
end of Bk. II and beginning of Bk. III.   Bibl.: Coxe, Greek MSS., cols 232–5. Wilson, pls. 56–7.

MS. Barocci 133

66. Miscellany.   13th cent.

As well as works by Aristides, Libanios and Synesios, this volume contains two
essays by Julian the Apostate, whose writings were not systematically destroyed by
the Christians, as might have been expected. Fol. 27ʳ shows the beginning of his Misopogon.

Later history: the volume first appears in Bodleian lists c. 1655. Bibl.: Coxe, Greek MSS., Misc. 57. S.C. 3561. **MS. Auct. E. 4. 12**

67. Minor Attic orators. Early 14th cent.

Manuscripts of these orators (Lycurgus, Antiphon, Dinarchus) are not common. The most important is the codex Crippsianus in the British Library, MS. Burney 95, which is of much the same date as the present exhibit. It is curious that there is so little trace of these authors before the period known as the Palaeologan Renaissance (1261–c.1340). The scribe of this book is also found in MS. Vat. gr. 626, dated 1306.

Later history: Clermont → Meerman.   Bibl.: Coxe, Greek MSS., Misc. 208.   Page exhibited: fol. 16ᵛ, opening of Dinarchus, In Aristogeitonem.

MS. Auct. T. 2.8   PLATE VI

68. EURIPIDES. Early 14th cent.

This copy is typical of many texts of Greek drama: it contains the so-called 'triad', the three plays of the author in question that were standard reading in Byzantine schools. In the case of Euripides these were the Hecuba, Orestes and Phoenissae.

Bibl.: Coxe, Greek MSS., col. 199. Wilson pls. 64-5.

Pages exhibited: fols. 31ᵛ-32ʳ, part of the hypothesis of the Orestes and the beginning of the text, with interlinear glosses and marginal scholia.   MS. Barocci 120

69. APHTHONIUS and HERMOGENES. A.D. 1308

These rhetorical handbooks were much studied in Byzantium as guides to good prose style. This manuscript was copied by the famous scholar Demetrios Triklinios (see no. 84). It is the earliest of his dated, signed manuscripts.

Bibl.: Coxe, College MSS. Exh. Byz. 1966, no. 19.   Page exhibited: fol. 3ʳ, the beginning of Aphthonius.

New College, MS. 258

70. SOPHOCLES, etc. Early 14th cent.

The texts in this substantial corpus of ancient poetry were all part of the normal school curriculum. The manuscript is of no special importance except that it alone of the manuscripts of Sophocles gives the right reading at Ajax 330: λόγοις, written as a variant above the line (fol. 85ᵛ, exhibited, fourth line from the bottom). This is also known from a quotation in the Anthology of Stobaeus.

Later history: acquired by Laud in 1637.

Bibl.: Coxe, Greek MSS., cols. 536–8.

MS. Laud Gr. 54

71. PROCLUS, Platonic theology, Elements of theology. A.D. 1357/8

The manuscript was copied in 1357/8 by Stelianos Choumnos for Johannes Contostephanos from Constantinople. It belonged later to Giovanni Pica della Mirandola (1463–94) and Domenico Grimani (c. 1461–1523): perhaps the first example to come to light of a book containing both names.

Later history: acquired by Laud before or in 1633.

Bibl.: Coxe, Greek MSS., cols. 501–2. Exh. Byz. 1966 no. 54. Wilson, pl. 69 R.W. Hunt's introduction to Coxe, Laudian manuscripts, p. xviii n. 56.

Pages exhibited: fols. 241ᵛ–242ʳ, the end of the Platonic theology and beginning of the Elements of theology.

MS. Laud Gr. 18

72. PLUTARCH, Lives. A.D. 1362

A fine piece of calligraphy by Manuel Tzykandyles, a scribe active in Mistra, which was becoming a cultural centre of some importance at this date. The rest of the manuscript, with the scribe's colophon, is now in Milan, Bibl. Ambrosiana, MS. D 538 inf.

Bibl.: Coxe, Canonici MSS. Wilson, pl. 70.

Page exhibited: fol. 1ʳ, the beginning of the life of Theseus.

MS. Canon. Gr. 93

73-77. Reference Books

Some of the reference books needed by Greek scholars in the Middle Ages and Renaissance.

73. The Suda lexicon. 14th cent.

The Suda, a large compilation in alphabetical order put together in the 10th cent., combines the functions of dictionary and encyclopaedia of ancient culture. Fol. 30ʳ, exhibited, contains the beginning of entries under the letter Δ.

Later history: acquired in 1841.   Bibl.: Coxe, Greek MSS., Misc. 290.

MS. Auct. V. 1. 53

74. Lexicon (formerly ascribed to Cyril of Alexandria), etc. 12th cent.

This and the next exhibit show the two dictionaries most commonly used in Byzantium. Between fifty and a hundred manuscripts of each are known.

There is some reason to consider this copy the product of a scriptorium in southern Italy, and it is noteworthy that the same is true of a very large number of lexicographical manuscripts.

Bibl.: R. Barbour in B.L.R. 6(1960), 612-3.   Pages exhibited: fols. 73ᵛ-74ʳ, the end of entries under N and the beginning of Ξ.

MS. Holkham Gr. 112

75. ZONARAS, Lexicon. 13th cent.

The compiler of this work was a canon lawyer and historian.

Bibl.: Coxe, Canonici MSS. Wilson, pl. 55.   Pages exhibited: fols. 101ᵛ-102ᵃ, the end of entries under Δ and the beginning of E.

MS. Canon. Gr. 65

76. Specialised lexica, etc. Late 10th or 11th cent.

This little book, which may be another product from an Italian scriptorium, contains a number of lexica to individual authors. Fol. 94ʳ, exhibited, contains the beginning of a vocabulary list of Homer. Our plate (fol. 171ᵛ) shows the end of a similar glossary to the poems of St. Gregory of Nazianzus, and the beginning of a small treatise by the 6th-cent. grammarian John Philoponos on words which have different meanings according to their accentuation.

<u>MS. Gr. class. f. 114</u>   PLATE VIII(b)

77. Lexica.   15th cent.

Despite its late date this is an important collection. As well as some of the same items as in the preceding exhibits, it contains an abridgement of the etymological dictionary by the 5th-cent. grammarian Orion (see plate VII(a)), and it is the unique source of fr. 69 of Stesichorus (fol. 90ʳ, exhibited).

<u>Later history</u>: Meerman.   <u>Bibl.</u>: Coxe, Greek MSS., Misc. 211.

<u>MS. Auct. T. 2.11</u>   PLATE VII(a)

78-83. Grammars

Specimens of the grammars available to students of Greek.

78. ROGER BACON, Greek grammar.   14th cent.

Roger Bacon (c. 1214-94) was Grosseteste's most enthusiastic disciple in stressing the importance of studying Greek texts in the original. This is the only known copy of his grammar; it was written in England in the 14th cent. It is palimpsest, re-using parchment from a 13th-cent. copy of the Decretals. Pp. 10-11 show the Pater Noster, Ave Maria, and Creed written successively in Greek, Greek transliterated, and Latin.   Later history: from the bequest of Brian Twyne, 1644. Probably belonged earlier to John Dee.

Bibl.: Coxe, College Mss.   Exh. Byz. 1966, no. 39.   Corpus Christi College, MS. 148

79. Greek grammarians.   13th cent.

A substantial collection of grammatical treatises. Fol. 44ᵛ, exhibited, contains the beginning of the most famous of all, the short Ars grammatica by Dionysius Thrax (title on line 2). This text seems to have been the basis of grammatical instruction in the schools of late antiquity and Byzantium; it also achieved the distinction of being translated into Syriac and Armenian. The untidy script in this manuscript is typical of that used by schoolmasters and scholars in the 13th cent.

Bibl.: Coxe, Greek Mss., cols. 192-4.   MS. Barocci 116

80. MANUEL MOSCHOPOULOS, grammar. Late 15th cent.

The author was one of the leading scholars in Byzantium c. 1300. Fol. 92ʳ, exhibited, contains the beginning of his declension tables.   Later history: Soranzo (foliation of the typical sort).

Bibl.: Coxe, Canonici Mss.   MS. Canon. Gr. 11

81. MANUEL CHRYSOLORAS, Erotemata.   Late 15th cent.

The author was the first person to give regular Greek lessons in the West; he lectured in Florence from 1397 onwards. His book enjoyed enormous popularity and was the first Greek grammar to be printed. Fol. 12ʳ, exhibited, contains the beginning of the conjugation of τύπτω, which he took as his model of the standard Greek verb, despite the fact that most of its forms are not attested in Attic Greek. Many later grammars repeated this error.

Later history: Soranzo (typical binding and floral endpapers).

Bibl.: Coxe, Canonici Mss.   MS. Canon. Gr. 26

82. MANUEL CHRYSOLORAS, Erotemata.   16th cent.

Another copy of the preceding. Fol. 30ʳ exhibits the opening chapter, on the alphabet.

Bibl.: Coxe, Greek MSS., cols. 10-12.   MS. Barocci 6

83. CONSTANTINE LASCARIS, etc.   Late 15th cent.

A volume of treatises in which the final item is by Constantine Lascaris (1434 — 1501), a Greek refugee who taught for a while in Milan and then moved to Messina. The scribe also wrote a famous copy of grammatical treatises now in Copenhagen (GKS 1965). Our manuscript contains hitherto unnoticed marginalia by Constantine Lascaris himself (e.g. on fols. 140ʳ, exhibited, and 151ʳ, reproduced in plate).

Later history: Saibante.   Bibl.: Coxe, Greek MSS, Misc. 245.

MS. Auct. T. 4.7   PLATE VII (b)

84-87. The Renaissance

Copies of Greek authors (other than Homer) from the Renaissance.

84. ARISTOPHANES.   Early 15th cent.

Eight plays (the surviving works apart from Lys., Thesm., Eccl.). This copy incorporates the recension by Demetrios Triklinios (see no. 69), in which he exploited his expert metrical knowledge.

Bibl: R. Barbour in B.L.R. 6 (1960), 609.   Wilson, pl. 73.   Page exhibited: fol. 73ʳ, beginning of the Frogs.

MS. Holkham Gr. 88

85. Ps.-APOLLODORUS, Bibliotheca.   15th cent.

The earliest complete manuscript. It was copied from Paris gr. 2722 before half of it was lost. Bound up with others, it belonged to cardinal Bessarion, who gave it to S. Marco, Venice (no. 478 in the catalogue of 1468).

Later history: acquired by Laud in 1636.   Bibl.: Coxe, Greek MSS., col. 538. Exh. Byz. 1966, no. 51.

Pages exhibited: fol. v^v, Bessarion's autograph ex-libris in Greek and Latin, and fol. 1a^r, the beginning of the text, with Laud's

ownership inscription.   MS. Laud Gr. 55

86. ISOCRATES.   15th cent.

The scribe of this book, Girard of Methone, is known to have worked in Mantua c. 1430; he was perhaps employed specifically as Greek copyist at the Gonzaga court. A great many manuscripts written by him were not recognized until recently, owing to the variable appearance of his hand. Several have cryptographic colophons, one type of which is illustrated in plate VIII (a).

Bibl.: Coxe, Canonici MSS. N. G. Wilson in Revue d'histoire des textes, 4 (1975, forthcoming).   PLATE VIII(a).

Page exhibited: fol. 71^v, the opening of the Panathenaicus.   MS. Canon. Gr. 87

87. EUSTRATIUS and others, Commentaries on ARISTOTLE, Nicomachean Ethics.   A.D. 1495

Very few Greek manuscripts were written in England in the 15th cent. This example is signed and dated by John Serbopoulos, a refugee from Constantinople, who tells us that he was writing 'in a village called Reading' (plate X).

The manuscript bears on its front paste-down the ex-libris of William Grocyn (c. 1449 - c. 1519), who gave the first public lectures on Greek in Oxford University, c. 1491-3.

Bibl.: Coxe, College MSS.   Page exhibited: fol. 1^r, the opening of the commentary of Eustratius (12th-cent.).

Corpus Christi College, MS. 106.   PLATE X

Latin
88-92. Subscriptions

In a number of classical works subscriptions are found stating that the texts have been written out, or checked, or simply read by particular individuals. Checking was carried out sometimes against other copies (nos. 88-89), sometimes with the help of a teacher (no. 92), even without help of any kind. The names take us back to the age of Symmachus and show that members of the senatorial class were involved. The practice of entering subscriptions was carried over into Christian texts, and continued until the third quarter of the 6th cent. Half-a-dozen subscriptions survive in originals, such as that found in the 'Mediceus' of Vergil (see no. 28), but the majority, including all those shown here, survive because they were taken over by later copyists as part of the text. The first Decade of Livy (no. 88) is an example of a textual tradition where all the extant manuscripts, except a scrap of papyrus (no. 49) and a palimpsest (C.L.A. IV, no. 499), descend from a copy put together in the circle of Symmachus; this is a case where the one copy that survived the Dark Ages came from a distinguished library. For Rufinus' translation of Gregory of Nazianzus (no. 89), the subscription implies a connection with the circle of Rufinus himself, but the manuscripts which carry it have little importance for the transmission of the text.

The subscription in the 9th-cent. Priscian (no. 90, pl. XI) appears closely to reflect the physical appearance of the 6th-cent. original. That in the

· 12th-cent. Caesar (no. 91, pl. XII) has been transformed in style into a Romanesque design, and those in the 14th-cent. Cassian (no. 92) are written as part of the text.

88. LIVY, First decade.   First half of the 11th cent.

Written in Eastern France, to judge from the style of the initials. The subscription, on fol. 83ᵛ (exhibited. Plate X(a)) has become a little corrupt. The scribe wrote DEXTERVM instead of DEXTER V.C.

Later history: Clermont → Meerman.

Bibl.: S.C. 20631. Pächt & Alexander, i no. 435. New Pal. Soc., 1st Ser., pls. 165-6. R.M. Ogilvie, ed., O.C.T. 1974, p. xii (siglum O).

MS. Auct. T. I. 24   PLATE X(a)

89. GREGORY of NAZIANZUS, Apologeticus and Orations, translated by Rufinus of Aquileia.   First half of the 9th cent.

Written at the abbey of Lorsch, near Worms. At the end of Or. VII (fol. 63ʳ, exhibited. Plate X(b)) is the subscription ' Usque huc contuli de codicae (sic) sanctae Melaniae Roma'. This refers to St. Melania the elder (c. 342 - c. 410), who had been closely associated with Rufinus in founding a double monastery on the Mount of Olives, and who returned to Rome in 399 or 400. But in spite of the authority implied by the subscription, the text of this manuscript contains 'inmumerae lectiones falsae' (Engelbrecht, p. LX).

Later history: Lorsch → Eberbach (?) → Laud.   Bibl.: Coxe, Laudian manuscripts, cols. 226-7, p. 555.

Edition of A. Engelbrecht, C.S.E.L., 46 (1910), esp. xxx-xxxiii, LX-LXI. Bischoff, Lorsch im Spiegel..., 41, 88, 100-101.

MS. Laud Misc. 276   PLATE X(b)

90. PRISCIAN, Institutiones grammaticae.   Second half of the 9th cent.

The subscription exhibited on fol. 135ᵛ (plate XI), after Bk. XVI, records the copying of the work by Fl. Theodorus, a chancery official and pupil of Priscian, in Constantinople, A.D. 526-7. Similar subscriptions by the same man occur before Bk. VI (fol. 45ʳ), before Bk. IX (fol. 87ᵛ), and after Bk. XVII (fol. 156ᵛ).

The manuscript contains numerous glosses, near-contemporary, including a few in Old High German.

Later history: Clermont → Meerman.   Bibl.: S.C. 20622. H. Mayer, *Althochdeutsche Glossen: Nachträge*, Toronto 1975, 108.

<u>MS. Auct. T. 1. 26</u>   PLATE XI

91. CAESAR, <u>De bello Gallico</u>.   First half of the 12th cent.

The Julius Celsus of the subscription (fol. 128ᵛ, exhibited. Plate XII) is unknown. In the Middle Ages he was sometimes regarded as the author of the <u>De bello Gallico</u>. This manuscript was written probably in the Low Countries.

Later history: belonged in the 15th cent. to the abbey of Egmond in the diocese of Utrecht (fol. iiiᵛ, note of repair by abbot Gherardus Poelgheest, 1465). It is the Codex Egmondanus of Oudendorp (see V. Brown, *The textual transmission of Caesar's Civil War* [Mnemosyne, suppl. 23], Leiden 1972, 5 n.1). Bookplate of Thomas William Coke.

<u>MS. Holkham misc. 34</u>   PLATE XII

92. CASSIAN, <u>De institutis coenobiorum</u> and <u>Collationes</u>.   Early 14th cent.

At the end of <u>Inst.</u> I (fol. 4ᵛ), II (fol. 8ʳ), III (fol. 10ᵛ) is the subscription 'Emendaui in monasterio Siluaniano cum Simplicio', and at the end of <u>Coll.</u> II (fol. 58ᵛ), III (fol. 63ᵛ, exhibited), V (fol. 73ʳ) and VIII (fol. 90ʳ) 'Contuli cum Gaudentio in monasterio Siluaniano'. Neither the monastery nor the men have been identified. These subscriptions have been reported up to now only from this late manuscript, which contains French illumination on fol. 2ʳ, but was probably written by an Italian, on southern parchment with flourished initials in Italian style.

Later history: given by William Gray, bishop of Ely (d. 1479).

Bibl.: R.A.B. Mynors, *Catalogue of the manuscripts of Balliol College Oxford*, Oxford 1963, p. 291.

<u>Balliol College, MS. 275</u>

93-95. Ireland and England

The only early Anglo-Saxon manuscripts of classical texts to survive are now abroad: the Leiden fragment of Pliny's Natural History (C.L.A. x, no. 1578), the leaf of Justinus (C.L.A. ix, no. 1370), and the grammatical works at St. Paul in Carinthia (C.L.A. x, nos. 1451-3). For our exhibits, we have therefore had to resort to indirect evidence: later manuscripts of works which show the use of classical texts by the Irish and the English of the 7th and 8th centuries in works of practical scholarship on computus (no. 93) and grammar (no. 94, cf. no. 24) and for more teasing purposes (no. 95). These later continental copies illustrate in themselves the influence of Irish and English culture on the civilization of Europe.

93. Excerpts from MACROBIUS, Saturnalia, I. xii–xv.

1075, or shortly before.

This collection of excerpts on the origins of the Roman calendar is found here and in five earlier manuscripts in association with other works on computus, the art of calculating astronomical occurrences and the movable dates of the Christian calendar. Bede had access to a computistical miscellany containing these excerpts from Macrobius, but not to a complete text of the Saturnalia, for he quotes freely from the excerpts and not one word more. He shows knowledge of many of the other items found in this manuscript, some of which are also cited in a letter written by an Irish scholar Cummian, c. A.D. 632. The Macrobian excerpts seem to have been known to the Irish, for the oldest manuscript in which they survive (Vienna, Nationalbibl., Ser. nov. 37 = C.L.A. x, no. 1510) is said by E. A. Lowe to have been copied at Salzburg at the end of the 8th cent., apparently from an Irish exemplar for which the most likely source is Virgil of Salzburg (see no. 95). The Vienna fragment is earlier than any complete copy of the *Saturnalia* now extant.

Our manuscript was written at the Benedictine abbey of the Holy Trinity at Vendôme, in 1075 or shortly before.   Later history: Jacques Sirmond (1559-1651). E. Bernard.

Bibl.: S.C. 8837. L. Halphen, *Recueil d'annales angevines et vendômoises* (Collection de textes pour servir à l'étude et à l'enseignement de l'histoire), Paris 1903, xxv-xxxi, 50-79 ; C.W. Jones, 'The 'Lost' Sirmond Manuscript of Bede's 'Computus'', *English Historical Review*, 52 (1937), 204-219.

Page exhibited: fol. 101ʳ, the start of the Macrobian excerpts (they end on fol. 105ᵛ).

MS. Bodley 309   PLATE XIII (a)

94. Collection of grammatical treatises.   Early 11th cent.

The page exhibited (fol. 153ᵛ) contains a glossary of 45 Latin words, 31 of which are glossed in Old English. The language indicates a Mercian origin early in the 8th cent. The lemmata nos. 1-27 are mainly from Priscian and Donatus, but the remainder (nos. 28-45) are from an unidentified source, presumably grammatical.

The glossary had reached Italy by the early 11th cent. at latest, when it was transcribed here with many other grammatical texts. The script is Caroline minuscule, apparently written by a scribe trained in the Beneventan script, into which he occasionally lapses (see pl. XIV).

Later history : some accounts on fols. 168ᵛ-9ʳ, partly dated 1408, mention names, including 'Magistro F. de Fiano', probably to be identified as Francesco da Fiano, who spent at least 40 years, from c. 1379, as a member of the papal curia (see G. Billanovich in *Italia medioevale e umanistica*, 6 (1963), 211, 214-222). On fol. 168ʳ is the erased inscription 'domini Lelii de Valle' (= Della Valle). He was a lawyer and advocate in the papal consistory, and 'taxator litterarum apostolicarum' from 1455 until his death before Nov. 1476 (W. von Hofmann, *Forschungen zur Geschichte der Kurialen Behörden*, II, 1914, pp. 96, 162). By the 16th cent., the ms. had reached the Low Countries, where it was given its present blind-stamped binding. Bought by the Bodleian in 1825.

Bibl.: S.C. 28188. Pächt & Alexander, ii no. 5. For the glosses, see A.S. Napier in *Archiv für das Studium der neueren Sprachen*, 85 (1890),

309-316, and in his Old English glosses (Anecdota Oxoniensia, *Mediaeval and Modern Series*, XI), Oxford 1900, XXI-XXII, 218-9.

A detailed description of the contents of the whole manuscript is to be published by C. Jeudy in *Viator*. A palaeographical study

is being undertaken by F. Newton, who first drew our attention to the Beneventan features.

<u>MS. Add. C. 144</u>   PLATE XIV

95. 'AETHICUS ISTER', <u>Cosmographia</u>.   Late 8th cent.

This is a fictitious geography which claims the authority of St. Jerome (see the title exhibited on fol. 2ʳ). Among the sources used is Pomponius Mela, whose work only survived into the Middle Ages in one ancient exemplar made at Ravenna in the 6th cent., now represented by a direct copy written under the direction of Heiric of Auxerre (841-876/7), Vat. lat. 4929. The author of the <u>Cosmographia</u> has been identified as the Irishman St. Virgil (i.e. Fergal) of Salzburg, the 'Apostle of Carinthia' (c. 700-784), see no. 93. Unfortunately this identification cannot be regarded as proven. However, it seems likely that the work was composed by an Irishman on the continent.

We show an early copy, written 'in the Germanic area, in a centre under Insular influence' (E. A. Lowe).   <u>Bibl.</u>: S.C. 5137. Pächt & Alexander, i, no. 1. C.L.A. II, 2nd ed., no. 242.

<u>Later history</u>: by the 15th cent., bound up in a composite volume in the library of Murbach (Alsace). M. Z. Boxhorn (1612-1653).

F. Junius (1589-1677), who gave his collection to the University of Oxford.   <u>MS. Junius 25, fols. 2-59</u>

96-99. The Carolingian Age

The Carolingian revival was the decisive period in the transmission of Latin texts, and secured their survival. The way in which texts were sought out and copied is not directly recorded, but recently Bernhard Bischoff has shown how evidence for the work of the Palace library under Charlemagne and under Louis the Pious can be found, and has identified manuscripts which can reasonably be regarded as products of its scriptorium (see no. 96). He has also pointed to the way in which the growth of libraries of the great abbeys can be connected with the court of the Emperors. Our examples are mostly connected with Lorsch, an abbey founded in 764, richly endowed and favoured by Charlemagne and his successors. No. 98 is one of the few instances of a Carolingian manuscript which can be confronted with a surviving ancestor.

Bibl.: B. Bischoff, 'Die Hofbibliothek Karls des Großen' in Karl der Große, Lebenswerk und Nachleben (ed. W. Braunfels).

II, Das geistige Leben (ed. B. Bischoff), Düsseldorf 1965, 42-62.

96. SIDONIUS APOLLINARIS, Letters.   First half of the 9th cent.

The manuscripts of this text go back to a single archetype which was slightly damaged at the beginning. The most faithful and literal copy of it is our manuscript in which blank spaces were left for the gaps in the text (see fol. 4^v, exhibited. Plate XV). Bischoff has suggested the possibility that this manuscript was written in the Palace School of Louis the Pious (814-840). The script is a magnificent example of Caroline minuscule.   Later history: Lorsch (?) → Eberbach → Laud (1638).

Bibl.: Coxe, Laudian manuscripts, col. 46 and pp. 541-2, and R. W. Hunt's introduction, pp. xxiv-xxv. Ellis I, pls 2-3 (fols. 71^r-72^r)

and II, pl. 3 (fol. 74^r). F. Leo's introduction to the edition of C. Luetjohann in M.G.H., Auctores antiquissimi VIII, Berlin

1887, esp. pp. XXVII-XLI. P. Mohr, ed., Teubner, Leipzig 1895, IV-VII. B. Bischoff, Lorsch im Spiegel..., 50, 67, 79, 100-101.

MS. Laud Lat. 104   PLATE XV

97. SIDONIUS APOLLINARIS, Letters.   11th cent.

The lacunae of no. 96 are here filled in, as in other copies. The source of such supplements appears to have been another early manuscript used only for this purpose. No. 97 was certainly in England by the 14th cent., but its origin is uncertain.

Later history : bound up with other manuscripts in an early 17th-cent. binding stamped with the arms of Hatton of Holdenby.

From the collection of Christopher, 1st baron Hatton, purchased 1671.   Bibl.: S.C. 4056. Luetjohann (see no. 96), xx.

Page exhibited : fol. 115ʳ, containing the same passage as that shown in no. 96.   **MS. Auct. F. 5. 25, fols. 113-150**

98. AUGUSTINE, De baptismo paruulorum. First half of the 9th cent.

Written either at St. Vaast of Arras, or at Lorsch in the style of St. Vaast (Bischoff). The manuscript is closely related to an uncial manuscript of the early 7th cent. at the Escorial (C.L.A. XI, no. 1629). It is not a direct copy, but is certainly descended from it through at least one intermediary which incorporated a few readings from another source. Nevertheless, the Laudian manuscript is so close to the Escorialensis that it takes over marginal headings, and copies the ancient form of quire-signature (see fols. 254ᵛ - 255ʳ, exhibited).   Later history : Lorsch → Eberbach → Laud.

Bibl.: Coxe, Laudian manuscripts, cols. 131-2, and R.W. Hunt's introduction, pp. xxiv-xxv. M. Petschenig, ed., C.S.E.L., 51 (1908),

xlii-xxi. Bischoff, Lorsch im Spiegel..., 32, 34, 65, 77, 100-101.   **MS. Laud Misc. 130, fols. 207-298**

99. Fragment of CICERO, Tusculan Disputations (V. 114-120).   9th cent.

The penultimate leaf of the text from a manuscript copied in three columns, a format which is very rare, but ancient (cf. no. 108). It is hard to place such a small fragment in the textual tradition; there is a chance that it belongs to the important stream ('y') now represented only by contemporary corrections in the 9th-cent. Vat. lat. 3246 ('V') and by readings found in late and contaminated copies, but this cannot be confirmed because the corrector of V did not continue to the end of the text. In § 119 our manuscript reads 'obruantur' which had been conjectured by Bentley, where all the other manuscripts read 'obseruant' or the like.

Later history: once used as a paste-down; now bound up at the end of a composite volume, of which fols. 1-24 if not all

belonged to the Carthusians of Mainz and were acquired by Laud in 1638.

Bibl.: Coxe, Laudian manuscripts, col. 16 and p. 538, and R.W. Hunt's introduction, p. xxiv. A.C. Clark in Mélanges... É. Chatelain,

Paris 1910, 169-173, with plate. M. Pohlenz, ed. Teubner, Leipzig 1918, XVIII.   **MS. Laud Lat. 29, fol. 171**

100-106. France

The libraries of the great French abbeys housed some ancient manuscripts, although the future of these was precarious — for example, no. 104, a manuscript from the library of Fleury, was once part of a volume with fly-leaves from a 6th-cent. bible. But the upsurge in output of the French scriptoria during the 9th cent. was sufficient to save and diffuse most of the surviving relics of Latin literature. What we can show here is but a pale reflection of these activities. Nos. 100-101 illustrate the work of the great scholars of the Palace School at Laon; they were using Martianus Capella as a basic text. Nos. 102-3 are grammatical miscellanies perhaps from Auxerre, and no. 103 ends with Seneca's letters copied from a very battered exemplar. No. 104 shows the lighter moments of the students who worked from it at Fleury in the 10th and 11th centuries. In no. 106, a Macrobius from the end of the 10th cent., the baneful process of contamination is at work as a direct result of the excerpting tendencies of 9th-cent. scholars. No. 105 passed through the hands of Pierre Daniel, one of the 16th-cent. scholars whose collecting habits, though often ruthless, were instrumental in saving many French manuscripts as they emerged from their monastic fastnesses.

100. MARTIANUS CAPELLA, etc.   9th cent.

Martianus was one of the prime sources for the study of the seven liberal arts from the 9th cent. onwards. This manuscript was written in France, probably in the Loire valley. Its near-contemporary glosses are identified by J.G. Préaux as from the commentary which he attributes to the Irishman, Martin of Laon. The Song of the Muses ('Scande caeli templa ...', II. 117 sqq. Fols. 11ᵛ-12ʳ, exhibited) was set to music by the addition of neums. Such neums are found in medieval manuscripts of classical poets such as Lucan.

Later history: fol. 1ᵛ, 15th-cent. ownership (?) inscription, erased and not yet deciphered. Acquired by Laud before 1633 in a

group from an important, but still unidentified, French collection (fol. 1ʳ, the number ii ᶜ xxxiiii and paraph sign).

Bibl.: Coxe, Laudian manuscripts, cols. 53-4 and p. 542, and R. W. Hunt's introduction, pp. xvi – xvii. E. W. B. Nicholson,

Introduction to the study of some of the oldest Latin musical manuscripts ... (Early Bodleian Music, [3]), London 1913,

p. xxii, pls. X, XI (fols. 11ᵛ, 12ʳ). J. G. Préaux in Latomus 12 (1953), 439-440. C. Leonardi in Aevum 34 (1960), 423. S. Corbin

in Opera and English Music. Essays in honour of Sir Jack Westrup, Oxford (forthcoming), 1-7.

MS. Laud Lat. 118

101. JOHANNES SCOTTUS ERIGENA, Commentary on Martianus Capella.   2nd half of the 9th cent.

John the Scot (c. 810 - c. 877), an Irishman by birth, was made head of the Palace School at Laon by Charles the Bald. His commentary on Martianus was published in 1939 by C. E. Lutz from Paris lat. 12960, fols. 47-115; our manuscript, the only other complete copy, was discovered by L. Labowsky and presents a version which differs somewhat, especially in Bk. I (? an earlier version). John's commentary includes references to a 'Peplus Theophrasti', a lost work known only from references made by the 9th-cent. scholars of Laon (who studied Greek); that exhibited here on fol. 7ᵛ (on Martianus I. 10) does not appear in the Paris manuscript.

This manuscript was written in France and contains a damaged ex-libris of the abbey of St. Vincent at Metz, late 10th- or 11th-cent.

Later history: clermont → Meerman.   Bibl.: S. C. 20628 (see also corrections in vol. V, p. XVII).

On the commentary, see L. Labowsky in Mediaeval and Renaissance Studies, I (1941-3), 189-193, and C. E. Lutz in

Catalogus translationum et commentariorum (ed. P. O. Kristeller), II, Washington 1971, 371. On Theophrastus, see C. B.

Schmidt, ibid., p. 315, and H. Usener, 'Lectiones Graecae' in his Kleine Schriften I, Berlin 1912, 191-3.

MS. Auct. T. 2. 19

102. DONATUS, PRISCIAN, etc.   Third quarter of the 9th cent.

Written in the Auxerre area, or perhaps at Bourges. In the lower margin of
fol. 19ᵛ (shown), one of the anonymous glosses on Donatus, Ars maior (Keil IV, p.387)
proposes as examples of 'adverbs of place' 'Bituricae sum uel Autisiodori'.

Later history: Clermont → Meerman.   Bibl.: S.C. 20624. Pächt & Alexander, i, no. 418, pl. xxxiv (fol. 2ʳ).

C. Jeudy in Revue d'histoire des textes, 2 (1972), 117-8.   MS. Auct. T. 2. 20

103. Miscellany, including SENECA, letters 1–88 (fragmentary).
10th cent. (possibly end of the 9th).

Five of the works in this miscellany, including the 'extract form' of Nonius
Marcellus' De conpendiosa doctrina and the four astronomical excerpts from
Pliny's Nat. Hist. Bk. II (see no. 107), are also to be found in a late 9th-cent.
manuscript now divided into several pieces (Berne 347 + 357 + 330 + Paris lat. 7665
+ Leiden Voss. Lat. Q. 30, fols. 57-8). Both manuscripts contain many
grammatical texts, but each is distinguished by rare classical works not
appearing in the other: the Berne corpus contains the earliest extant copy
of Petronius' Excerpta uulgaria, and the Oxford manuscript has this early
copy of Seneca's letters 1–88. Although important, the text of Seneca is here
'so jumbled and fragmentary that the exemplar from which it was copied
could have been little more than a bundle of rags' (L.D. Reynolds, p. 25).

The Berne corpus was probably written at Auxerre, and it seems likely that
the Oxford volume also originated there. In the margin of fol. 39ᵛ, a name has
been added in the elongated letters of a contemporary chancery hand: 'Prodagius
clericus'.   Later history: the manuscript underwent some destructive process which caused purple stains,

and many leaves were lost (a stray quire is now at Leiden). Our section had reached Italy by the 15th cent.

Bibl.: Coxe, Canonici MSS. Pächt & Alexander, i, no. 425. E. Chatelain, 'Un nouveau manuscrit des lettres de Sénèque dispersé

entre Leyde et Oxford', Revue de Philologie, N.S. 21 (1897), 50-57, and in Paléographie des classiques latins, II, Paris 1894-1900, *p. 23, pl. CLXXII (Oxford, fol. 63ᵛ; Leiden, fol. 72ᵛ). L. D. Reynolds, The medieval tradition of Seneca's letters, Oxford 1965, esp. 152.*

Pages exhibited : fols. 63ᵛ-64ᵛ.   **MS. Canon. Class. Lat. 279** (+ Leiden, Voss. Lat. F. 70. I, fols. 67-73)

104. SOLINUS.   Late 9th or early 10th cent.

Not used in Mommsen's standard edition (2nd ed., Berlin 1895). The manuscript bears many early marks of Fleury ownership, including two 11th-cent. ex-libris (fols. 41ᵛ-42ʳ). The pages exhibited, fols. 42ᵛ-43ʳ, show the tendency of pupils at Fleury in the 10th and 11th centuries to scribble in their books: drawings, pen-trials, mirror-writing, neums, cryptographic writing, etc.

Later history : the last page (fol. 43ᵛ) bears a table of contents in the well-known hand of a Fleury librarian, late 12th-cent., showing that by then this book was the last part of a composite volume. The other sections, split up between the departure from the Collège de Clermont in 1764 and the Meerman sale of 1824, are now Berlin (East), Phill. 1833 + Phill. 1780 + The Hague, Museum Meermanno-Westreenianum 10 B I (fly-leaves, from a 6th-cent. bible, see C.L.A. VI, no. 799 and X, p. 38). According to our files, the first person to notice these connections with the Oxford manuscript seems to have been F. M. Carey in 1933.   *Bibl.: S.C. 20629. Pächt & Alexander i, no. 426.*   **MS. Auct. T. 2. 28**

105. MAXIMIANUS, Elegies, etc.   11th cent.

Attached to the Elegies is a little group of poems by more than one anonymous author of the 6th cent. They are also found in a few other manuscripts of Maximianus (see no. 139). Pierre Daniel added variants from an 'alt(er) v(etus) cod(ex)' (see fol. 13ᵛ) and supplied the remainder on a replacement leaf (fol. 15a ʳ⁻ᵛ, recto exhibited) and on the first leaf of the next section (fol. 16ʳ). That section (fols. 16 - ?23) is a separate manuscript which contains observations on the appearance in the sky of certain constellations in relation to the buildings of a monastery, perhaps St.-Aignan at Orléans. Pierre Daniel was responsible for the present binding of the composite volume, and it is uncertain whether the various sections were together before then. Most of Daniel's manuscripts came from abbeys in the area of the Loire valley.

<u>Later history</u>: Nicholas Heinsius → Edward Bernard.   <u>Bibl.</u>: <u>S.C.</u> 8849. Ellis <u>III</u>, pl. 20(fol. 6^{r·v}). H.W. Garrod

in <u>Classical Quarterly</u>, 4 (1910), 263-6. W. Schetter, <u>Studien zur Überlieferung und Kritik des Elegikers Maximian</u>

(Klassisch-Philologische Studien, Heft 36), Wiesbaden 1970, <u>passim</u>. On the star time-table of fols. 19^v-23^v, see R. Poole

in <u>Journal of Theological Studies</u>, 16 (1914), 98-104.   <u>MS. Bodley 38, fols. 1-14</u> (+15a^r-16^r)

106. MACROBIUS, Commentary on the <u>Somnium Scipionis</u> of Cicero.

End of the 10th cent.

Like Martianus Capella, Macrobius' Commentary was one of the channels by which ancient science and philosophy were conveyed to the medieval world. About 230 medieval manuscripts survive (not counting excerpts). Astronomical excerpts from the Commentary are found in the same corpus of computistical material, formed early in the 9th cent., which includes the Pliny excerpts (see no. 107). Towards the end of the century, probably at Auxerre, those Macrobian excerpts inspired another modification of Macrobius' full text. The sections at the beginning and end, which include discussions of dreams, the theory of numbers, the virtues, and the immortality of the soul, were jettisoned in favour of a slightly modified version of the central section, I.xiv, 21 — II.ix, 10, dealing with astronomy, musical theory, and world geography. The form became wide-spread in France and Germany in the 10th and 11th centuries, and even reached England in the 12th.

This French manuscript contains the short form of text as a nucleus, but it is being transformed back into the full form by injections from other textual streams; the process of replacing the missing passages had already begun in its exemplar, and was continued after the completion of this copy. In the opening exhibited (fols. 28^v-30^r), passages characteristically omitted in the short form have been supplied in the margins and on an extra slip of parchment (fol. 29^{r·v}).

This is a fine example of contamination, the mingling of different textual streams.

Plate XIII (b) shows one of three damaged leaves which were repaired by a near-contemporary scribe. The readings given on the added patches are so different from those of the received text that the repairer must have thought them up from his own head. They are to be considered in the light of a major question which confronts the modern textual critic : how good were medieval scribes at emending texts ?

There are extensive annotations by several early readers ; one of them added a set of glosses which is found in a number of other manuscripts of the full text from the 10th and 11th centuries, and which includes many quotations from classical and later authors.

Later history: Clermont → Meerman. By the time it was at the Collège de Clermont in the 18th cent., it was bound

up with an independent manuscript (fols. 51-98) of Macrobius' Saturnalia which had belonged to the abbey

of St. Vincent at Metz. At the Meerman sale it was purchased by Payne & Foss, to the fury of Sir Thomas Phillipps,

and was purchased from them by the Bodleian.

Bibl.: S.C. 20637 . Pächt & Alexander i. 430, pl. xxxv (fol. 1ʳ), cf. 431. MS. 'D' in the edition of J. Willis, Teubner, Leipzig 1963.

MS. Auct. T. 2. 27, fols. 1-50   PLATE XIII (b)

107-111. Germany (mainly).

During the period of the Ottonian emperors, the German schools were important, and played a considerable part in our story, not always sufficiently recognised.

107. HYGINUS, Astronomica.   End of the 10th, or early 11th cent.

The last two quires (fols. 25-38) of this copy of Hyginus are palimpsest. The lower script seems scarcely earlier than the upper, and the format is almost the same, so these leaves were probably waste in the scriptorium. Only a few words of the lower text can now be read, but the ultra-violet lamp reveals two diagrams (fol. 28ᵛ, pl. XVI, and fol. 31ʳ), which usually accompany astronomical excerpts from Pliny, Nat. Hist., Bk. II. The excerpts are found very frequently with a corpus of computistical material originally put together early in the century, though the graph diagram is a later addition of which the earliest examples occur in our no. 103, fol. 33ᵛ, and in Berne 347, fol. 24ᵛ.

MS. D'Orville 77, containing works of Cicero and Macrobius' commentary on the Somnium Scipionis (full text), was originally part of the same manuscript as the Hyginus. It was written in southern Germany, but an immediate ancestor of at least two of the works in MS. 77, Cicero's De senectute and the Macrobius, must have been brought there from France, perhaps from Corbie. Another closely related German manuscript of the 11th cent. is Munich, Clm 6369, which reached Munich with the Freising collection.

Later history: Isaac Verburg's sale, Amsterdam 1746, lot 486 (the two parts still together) → D'Orville.

Bibl.: S.C. 16955 + 16973. Ellis II, pl. 4 (fol. 6ᵛ) and III, pl. 13 (fol. 6ᵛ). Pächt & Alexander, i, nos. 27+28, pl. III (MS. 77, fols. 53ʳ and 113ᵛ). For the Pliny excerpts, see K. Rück, Auszüge aus der Naturgeschichte des C. Plinius Secundus... (Programm des Königlichen Ludwigs-Gymnasiums ... 1887/8), Munich 1888, and V. H. King, An investigation of some astronomical excerpts from Pliny's Natural History..., Oxford B.Litt. thesis, 1969. G.S. Vogel, The major manuscripts of Cicero's De senectute, 1939, 46-54. B.C. Barker-Benfield in Medieval learning and literature. Essays presented to R.W. Hunt (ed. J.J.G. Alexander & M.T. Gibson), Oxford 1975 (forthcoming), 160-162. Page exhibited: MS. 95, fol. 28ᵛ.

MS. D'Orville 95 (+ MS. D'Orville 77)   PLATE XVI

108. BOETHIUS, Logical commentaries; ALCUIN, De dialectica; CICERO, De inventione, glossed, with the commentary of Victorinus.
First half of the 11th cent.

A collection of texts for the study of logic and rhetoric, written out on an unusually lavish scale. Doubtless made in some important centre in southern Germany.

Later history: acquired in 1637 by Laud during his great acquisition of manuscripts from Germany.

Bibl.: Coxe, Laudian manuscripts, cols. 24-6, and R.W. Hunt's introduction, p. xxiv. Pächt & Alexander, i, no. 30, and pl. IV (fol. 29ᵛ). G. Lacombe et al., Aristoteles Latinus, I, Rome 1939, pp. 396-7 no. 336. L. Minio-Paluello in Mediaeval and Renaissance Studies, I (1941-3), 158, says that for the text of the Ps.-Boethian translation of Aristotle's Categories on fols. 29ʳ-32ᵛ it is a twin of Munich, Clm 18480, an 11th-cent. MS. with a 15th-cent. Tegernsee ex-libris. On the De inventione glosses, see M. Dickey in Mediaeval and Renaissance Studies, 6 (1968), 1-41, esp. 2.

Page exhibited: fol. 97ᵛ, the beginning of Cicero's Topica, with a note in a 15th-cent. which may be recognizable (plate XVII).

MS. Laud Lat. 49, fols. 1-166   PLATE XVII

109. TERENCE.   First half of the 11th cent.

The six comedies of Terence did not have the same place in education in the Middle Ages as they did in the 18th cent., but were nevertheless widely available. This glossed copy, written in Germany, is a school book like the D'Orville Horace (no. 110), and bears an 11th-cent. inscription at the end (fol. 112ᵛ) 'Adelheit. Hedwich. Matthilt. curiales adulescentulae unum par sunt amiciciae.   Page exhibited: fol. 93ᵛ, beginning of the Phormio.

Later history: lent by an Augsburg (?) monastery to Michael von Pfullendorf (Kammergerichtsschreiber to King Frederick III in 1444), see fol. 1ʳ. H.G. Ebner's sale, Nuremberg 1813, no. 384. Bought from Payne & Foss in 1819.

Bibl.: S.C. 28117. Pächt & Alexander, i no. 29. P. Wessner, ed., Aeli Donati ... commentum Terenti, III, Teubner, Leipzig 1908, XIII-XIV.

MS. Auct. F. 6. 27

110. HORACE, Opera.   Second half of the 11th cent.

A school book, written in the Mosan region, to judge from the initial (fol. 43ʳ). The text is contaminated. Among the early additions are pieces on the monochord and on fractions, also found, for example, in an 11th-cent. manuscript from

Tegernsee, MS. Lyell 57. The contemporary glosses include some in Old High German (fols. 6ᵛ, 8ᵛ exhibited, 51ʳ, 70ᵛ, 80ʳ).

Later history : notes in several later Italian hands, including a few in a gothic cursive probably of the late 14th cent.
(e.g. fols. 40ᵛ, 119ᵛ) and many in a thin humanistic cursive of the late 15th or early 16th cent. (see pl. XVIII(a) and fol. 9ʳ, exhibited) similar to the hand of the Neapolitan Janus Parrhasius (1470–1522), though the identification is not certain (cf. his annotations in Bodl. printed book 4° G 33 Art. BS., Terentius Scaurus etc., Pesaro 1511, with ex-libris of Antonius Seripandus 'ex Iani Parrhasii testamento'). Bought by D'Orville in Italy.

Bibl. : S.C. 17036. Pächt & Alexander, i, no. 267, pl. XVIII (fol. 43ʳ), with bibliography. F. Klingner, 2nd ed., Teubner, Leipzig 1950, p. xxi. For the OHG glosses, see E. Steinmeyer & E. Sievers, Die althochdeutschen Glossen, IV, Berlin 1898, pp. 334 and 588.   <u>MS. D'Orville 158</u>   PLATE XVIII(a)

111. HORACE, <u>Opera</u>.   Early 12th cent.

'Ex Britannicis [codicibus], quos omnes ipsi oculis usurpauimus, palmam facile aufert Codex Collegii Reginensis Oxonii...'. This judgement of Bentley long influenced editors of Horace, but it is now recognised that the manuscript presents a contaminated text. The late Eduard Fraenkel informed us that the text was closest to London, Brit. Libr., MS. Harl. 2725, a 9th-cent. copy apparently bought by J. G. Graevius at Cologne.

The 15th-cent. formal humanistic hand which added copious notes, including some in Greek (e.g. on fol. 5ᵛ, exhibited = plate XVIII(b)), is identifiable as that of Robert Flemmyng (<u>d</u>. 1483), who was nephew of the founder of Lincoln College, Oxford, and who studied in Italy.

History: country of origin uncertain, possibly English (see also the late 12th-cent. hand which added the list of contents on fol. 161ᵛ). Doubtless in England by the 14th cent., when an English hand added the note on fol. 83ʳ, now erased. The manuscript was among those which Flemmyng gave to Lincoln College in 1465, for it is identifiable from its 2° folio, <u>uidimus</u>, as no. 85 in the 1474 library catalogue (see R. Weiss in <u>B.Q.R.</u> 8 (1937), 350). It was given to Queen's College in 1595 by John Lloyd. Bentley borrowed the manuscript for at least three years, and had to be asked to return it (Hearne's diary 19 June 1706, ed. Oxford Historical Soc., 2 (1884), 263).

Bibl.: Coxe, College MSS. Richard Bentley's edition of Horace, I, Cambridge 1711, leaf c 2ᵛ. F. Klingner, 2nd ed., Teubner, Leipzig 1950, p. xxi. For Harl. 2725, see A.C. Clark in Classical Review, 5 (1891), 370. For Flemmyng's hand, see Exh. Duke Humfrey 1970, nos. 60-62 and p. 36.

Queen's College, MS. 202   PLATE XVIII (b)

112-116. Italy, 11th and 12th centuries.

There are few more difficult problems in the history of the transmission of ancient literature than to define the part played by Italian centres in the early Middle Ages. To what extent did manuscripts remain in Italy, to what extent were copies brought back after the Carolingian revival? The Juvenal (no. 113) is a case in point; the main text is of the vulgate type, but the unique lines were most probably derived from an Italian source. The Eton College manuscript (no. 114) is an early example of a common European collection of school texts, but certain features in some of the items have caused scholars to speculate about special Italian sources. No. 94, on the other hand, is an early 11th-cent. Italian manuscript which definitely incorporates some imported material.

Nos. 112-5 are in Beneventan script, all except no. 113 of the Bari type.

112. VERGIL, with marginal comm. including Servius.   Second half of the 11th cent.

Written in south Italy in a Beneventan hand of Bari type, with fine initials also akin to manuscripts from Bari (see fol. 123ʳ, exhibited). A number of missing leaves were replaced, probably in the early 14th cent.

A note in the manuscript by Canonici says that it once contained an
earlier note, removed before he acquired it, written by a certain 'N. Beccaria
Notaio Veronese che viveva nel principio del secolo xv' in which he said that
he had acquired it from the Alighieri family, and for this reason believed it
to be the manuscript used by Dante. According to Canonici, Beccaria left
this and other precious manuscripts to the canons of San Leonardo. Is 'N.
Beccaria' the Veronese humanist Antonio Beccaria (d. 1474) who made a
'donatio inter uiuos' of his manuscripts to the Lateran Canons of San Leonardo
outside Verona in April 1464, on condition that he could use them during his
lifetime? No. 12 among the manuscripts listed there was 'Virgilii opera
uetustissima cum comento Seruii circumquaque inscripto'. Some 15th-cent.
annotations in the manuscript, including passages of Greek, may be in
Beccaria's hand (e.g. fols. 7ʳ, 14ʳ, 15ʳ).

However, although the manuscript bears many notes in hands of the 13th
and 14th centuries, the Alighieri/Dante association is dubious. For one thing,
a 14th-cent. annotator, whose distinctive marginalia are particularly noticeable
on some of the replacement leaves with their otherwise blank margins (between
fols. 129–142), closely echoes the style of the Neapolitan jurist Pietro Piccolo
da Monteforte (c. 1307 – before 1384), admirer of Petrarch and friend of
Boccaccio. The annotations strongly recall those in the Valerius Maximus, Vat.
lat. 1919, reproduced and described by Billanovich. They include pointing hands,
and elegant drawings of a young man's head in profile (fol. 138). The annotations
in Milan, Ambros., C. 90 inf., an 11th-cent. Seneca from Montecassino, appear
to be in the same hand, as do the copious marginalia found in our MS. Auct.
F. 4. 30 (S.C. 8867), Ovid's _Metamorphoses_, 12th-cent.

On the verso of the last leaf of our Vergil, erased, is 'Liber J [aco]bi [Curu?]li
Ianuensis', written in a fine 15th-cent. humanistic cursive. This must be the

ex-libris of the Genoese humanist and diplomat, Giacomo Curlo, died c. 1459, a distinguished humanistic scribe who was official 'scriptor' in Naples to King Alfonso from 1445–1458.

Bibl.: Coxe, *Canonici MSS.* Pächt & Alexander, ii, no. 12, pl. II (fol. 113ᵛ). E. A. Lowe, 'Virgil in South Italy', reprinted from *Studi medievali*, 1932, in his *Palaeographical Papers 1907–1965*, ed. L. Bieler, Oxford 1972, I. 331-2, pl. 52 (fol. 7ʳ, shows the 15th-cent. Greek). For Antonio Beccaria and the inventory of his books, see G. P. Marchi in *Università di Padova, Facoltà di Lingue in Verona, Annali*, Ser. II, 1 (1966-7), 55-95. For his hand see also *Exh. Duke Humfrey* 1970, nos. 7-8. For annotations by Pietro Piccolo see G. Billanovich in *Medioevo e Rinascimento. Studi in onore di Bruno Nardi*, I, Florence 1955, esp. 23-32 and pl. I. For the notes in the Beneventan Seneca see F. Steffens, *Lateinische Paläographie*, 2nd ed., Trier 1909, pl. 75; detail of the same page in Lowe, *Palaeog. Papers*, II, pl. 141. For Giacomo Curlo see especially T. De Marinis, *La biblioteca napoletana dei re d'Aragona* I, Milan 1952, pp. 13-15, 35 and *Supplemento* I, Verona 1969, pp. 34-7, 71-2; B. L. Ullman, *The origin and development of humanistic script*, Rome 1960, 96-8.   MS. Canon. Class. Lat. 50

113. JUVENAL.   End of the 11th or early 12th cent.

This is the famous Juvenal in which E. O. Winstedt, while an undergraduate at Oxford, discovered 36 lines of Satire VI not found in any other manuscript, 34 after line 365 and 2 more after line 373 (fols. 20ᵛ-21ʳ, exhibited. Plate XIX). There has been much controversy about their genuineness, but agreement that they are ancient. The remainder of the text is an undistinguished representative of the vulgate. It seems most likely that an earlier reader had access to an ancient copy in which he found these lines and that he copied them into the vulgate ancestor of this manuscript without collating the rest of the text (cf. nos. 96-97). The exact place where the manuscript was written is not known, but since the script is Beneventan, it must have been written in south Italy.   Bibl.: Coxe, *Canonici MSS.* Ellis, III, pl. 17. Pächt & Alexander, ii, no. 24, pl. II (fol. 56ʳ). E. O. Winstedt in *Classical Review*, 13 (1899), 201-5 and in *Juvenalis ad satiram sextam in codice Bodl. Canon. XLI additi* versus XXXVI, Oxford 1899, with pl. J.G.Griffith in Hermes, 91 (1963), 104-114, speculates further about its history.

MS. Canon. Class. Lat. 41   PLATE XIX

114. THEODULUS; MAXIMIANUS; STATIUS, Achilleis; OVID, Remedia amoris and Heroides; ARATOR. 11th cent.

A school book, written in the Bari type of Beneventan script. In the Heroides it is the earliest manuscript to give the ancient introductory distichs for V, VI and VII; their source is a great puzzle. The pre-eminence of this manuscript for the text of Maximianus is no longer accepted.

Later history: probably one of the group of manuscripts bought in Venice and given to the College by Sir Henry Wotton, provost 1624-39.   Bibl.: M.R.James, A descriptive catalogue of the manuscripts in the library of Eton College, Cambridge 1895, pp. 81-2. E.A.Loew (Lowe), The Beneventan Script, Oxford 1914, 17, 18, 152, 338. A.P. McKinlay, Arator, the codices (The Mediaeval Academy of America. Publication no. 43), Cambridge (Mass.), 1942, pp. 42-3 no. 69, pl. xxv (fol. 77ʳ). H.Dörrie, 'Untersuchungen zur Überlieferungsgeschichte von Ovids Epistulae Heroidum', pts. I and II, Nachrichten der Akademie der Wissenschaften in Göttingen, Philologisch-Historische Klasse, (1960), 113-230, 359-423.

For the Maximianus, see refs. under no. 105.   **Eton College, MS. 150**

115. Questions on the Octateuch.   First quarter of the 12th cent.

Written in the Bari type of Beneventan script. At the end of the manuscript (fols. 108ᵛ-109ᵛ), in a different but contemporary Bari hand, are entered two hymns, one by 'Melus presbiter et monachus', who can be identified with Melus, prior and later (by 1123) abbot of the Abbey of All Saints, near Bari, and also prior of St. Nicholas, Bari. On fol. 111ᵛ is an ex-libris of St. Nicholas, Bari, 12th- or 13th-cent.

The work belongs to a genre which goes back to St. Augustine. One of the special features of the work shown here, not generally found in works of this type, is the inclusion of classical quotations, e.g. the slightly free quotation from

Cicero, _Philippics_ IV. 11 on the page exhibited (fol. 101^r). The closest analogue to the Questions in print is a work printed among the spuria of Bede, which does not contain this quotation (P.L. 93, col. 422).

Bibl.: Coxe, _Canonici MSS._ Pächt & Alexander ii, no. 29, pl. III (fol. 82^v). E.A. Lowe, _Scriptura Beneventana_, Oxford 1929, II pl. LXXXV (fols. I^v, 108^v). Ps.-Bede: P.L. 93, cols. 233-495. F. Stegmüller, _Repertorium biblicum_, 1958, no. 10061, records another copy, incomplete, in Bodl. MS. Laud Misc. 394.

MS. Canon. Pat. Lat. 175

116. CICERO, _De inventione._   Second half of the 12th cent.

The text is prefixed by an extraordinary miniature, in which Cicero as consul in 63 B.C. hears the arguments of Cato Uticensis and Caesar in deciding the fate of the Catilinarian conspirators (fol. 1^r, exhibited. Plate XX(b)). Pächt & Alexander say that 'the miniature probably goes back indirectly to a late classical source', and compare the ivory handle of the Bargello fan. A companion volume is now Lucca, Biblioteca Governativa, MS. 1405, a copy of the _Rhetorica ad Herennium_ preceded by a miniature of Cicero and Sallust, in the same style, script and size.

The origin of this pair is uncertain, perhaps north Italy or southern France. Our volume had reached England by the 15th cent., as its annotations show.

Later history: bequeathed by Thomas Barlow (1607-1691).   Bibl.: S.C. 6480. Pächt & Alexander, ii, no. 1047.

MS. Barlow 40   PLATE XX(b)

117-121. England, 9th-11th centuries.

There are very few surviving manuscripts of secular authors from the later Anglo-Saxon period. They are chiefly school texts. No. 117 is the only fundamental manuscript of a classical author in this section and was preserved as a relic of St. Dunstan. No. 118 is part of one of the best-known Anglo-Saxon libraries, that of Leofric, bishop of Exeter.

117. OVID, Ars amatoria, I.   Late 9th cent.

A quire of ten leaves bound up in a volume of miscellaneous contents connected with St. Dunstan. The last leaf (fol. 47, exhibited) is a replacement in a hand that may be St. Dunstan's own. The original manuscript was probably written in Wales. There are some glosses in Old Welsh, and the 'syntax marks' (W. M. Lindsay's phrase) inserted as a help to construing are also a Welsh feature. This manuscript and the 9th-cent. French copy, Paris Lat. 7311, are the oldest manuscripts of the work, and they are closely related.   Later history: at Glastonbury by s. xv², 'in custodia fratris H. Langley', fol. 47ᵛ. Given as part of a foundation gift by Thomas Allen in 1601.

Bibl.: S.C. 2176. Pächt & Alexander, iii no. 17, pl. I, with bibliography. W. M. Lindsay, Early Welsh Script (St. Andrews University Publications, 10), 1912, 7-10, pl. II. Complete facsimile, ed. R. W. Hunt, Umbrae codicum occidentalium 4, Amsterdam 1961. E. J. Kenney in Classical Quarterly, N.S. 12 (1962), 1-31.

MS. Auct. F. 4. 32, fols. 37 - 47

118. PERSIUS, with gloss.   Second half of the 10th cent.

Written at St. Augustine's, Canterbury, in a superb English Caroline script. The text is closely related to Cambridge, Trinity College, O. 4. 10 (James 1241), either a twin or a copy. The manuscript was bequeathed by Leofric, bishop of Exeter 1046-72, to his Cathedral Library. It is bound up with a copy of Boethius, De consolatione philosophiae (fols. 1-77), a distinct codex but a companion volume of like origin and date.

Later history: given by the Dean and Chapter of Exeter Cathedral, 1602.

Bibl.: S.C. 2455. Pächt & Alexander, iii, no. 37, with bibliography. É. Chatelain, Paléographie des classiques latins,
II, Paris 1894-1900, p.10, pl. CXXVI (fol.79ʳ). Ellis I, pl. 5 (fol. 88ᵛ). Ellis II, pl. 6 (fol. 80ᵛ). G.R. Scott in
Classical Review, 4 (1890), 17-19, 241-7. T.A.M. Bishop, English Caroline minuscule, Oxford 1971, no.9.
Page exhibited: fol. 79ʳ, the opening page.   MS. Auct. F. I. 15, fols. 78-92

119. AVIANUS, with other fables.   Late 11th cent.

One part of a school book, written in England and now bound in
two volumes. The other volume (MS. Rawl. G. 57) contains Disticha
Catonis and the epitome of the Iliad in Latin verse. The annotations
of both include glosses in Old English (see G. 111, fol. 15ᵛ, shown).

Later history: G. 111, fol. 29ʳ, 'Johannes de Fenton (?)', 14th-cent. (?). Divided and bound by Thomas Rawlinson;
bought at his sale, 4 March 1733/4, lots 5 and 12, by his brother Richard (1690-1755), who bequeathed his
collection to the Bodleian.   Bibl.: S.C. 14836, cf. 14788. Napier, Old English Glosses (see
no. 94), no. 28, see p. xix. N.R. Ker, Catalogue of the manuscripts containing Anglo-Saxon, Oxford 1957,
pp. 427-8 no. 350. A. Guaglianone, ed., Aviani fabulae (Corpus scriptorum Latinorum Paravianum),
Turin 1958, p. xvii, says that the scholia in the Avianus appear to be derived from Paris lat. 5570 (s. 'x-xi',
belonged to Fleury). The fables on fols. 16ʳ-51ᵛ are printed from this manuscript by L. Hervieux, Les
fabulistes latins, 2nd ed., II, Paris 1894, 653-713, under the title 'ex Romulo Nilantii ortae fabulae
metricae...'.   MS. Rawl. G. 111 (+ MS. Rawl. G. 57)

120. WULFSTAN the Cantor, Narratio metrica de
sancto Swithuno, etc.   2nd half of the 11th cent.

This is an Anglo-Saxon school book, containing a miscellany of Latin
verse, probably from Sherborne and dating from about the time when Stephen
Harding (later a co-founder of Cîteaux) was a 'puer' there. The other contents
include Prudentius, Dittochaeum; Theodulus; Avianus; Persius; Phocas, De nomine

et uerbo; the Latin <u>Iliad</u>; Ps.-Ovid, <u>Nux</u>; Statius, <u>Achilleis</u>; Lactantius, <u>Phoenix</u>. On the page shown (fol. 11^r. Plate xx(b)) is the start of a vocabulary headed 'GLOSAE', independent of the text in the margins of which it is entered. The glosses were collected mainly from those on Aldhelm, <u>De laude uirginitatis</u>, and were put in alphabetical order, an illustration of W. M. Lindsay's view of the origin of glossaries. <u>Later history</u>: annotated by Leland and very likely the manuscript

seen by him at Sherborne. <u>Bibl.</u>: <u>S.C.</u> 2657. Pächt & Alexander, iii, no. 60. Ellis, II, pl. 9 (fol. 106^r),

III, pl. 12 (fol. 106^r). Napier, <u>Old English glosses</u> (see no. 94), no. 18B, and see p. xviii. N. R. Ker, <u>Catalogue of manuscripts containing Anglo-Saxon</u>, Oxford 1957, pp. 353-4 no. 295. For W. M. Lindsay's view on the origin of glossaries, see <u>Classical Quarterly</u> 11 (1917), 121-4.

<u>MS. Auct. F. 2.14</u> PLATE xx(a)

121. ISIDORE, <u>De natura rerum</u>; CICERO, <u>Somnium Scipionis</u>, with MACROBIUS' Commentary.

2nd half of the 11th cent.

Two distinct manuscripts, but written in the same scriptorium and probably designed to go together from the start. This is the oldest surviving copy of the <u>Somnium Scipionis</u> with Macrobius' Commentary to have been written in England.

<u>Later history</u>: 'Georgius Chudlegh, Walterus Struchlegh, Devonienses', 16th-cent., fol. 62^r. Given by sir Henry Savile in 1620.

<u>Bibl.</u>: <u>S.C.</u> 2186. Pächt & Alexander, iii, no. 62, pl. VII (fol. 53^v), with further references.

<u>Page exhibited</u>: fol. 17^r, beginning of the <u>Somnium Scipionis</u>.

<u>MS. Auct. F. 2. 20</u>

122–127. England, late 11th–12th centuries.

This section illustrates the high quality of workmanship in English scriptoria in the century after the Norman Conquest, and gives a glimpse of the use made of classical texts by certain English clerics. William of Malmesbury was the last monastic autodidact before the rise of the Schools.

122. Herbal; SEXTUS PLACITUS, De uirtutibus bestiarum in arte medicinae.
Late 11th cent.

Executed at the Abbey of Bury St. Edmunds, with illustrations throughout. Medical texts were one of the types of illustrated books that survived from late antiquity. The illustrations here are reminiscent of Anglo-Saxon drawings of the late 10th and early 11th centuries, and were probably copied from a prototype of that period. We show the lively drawing of a horse at the beginning of the text of Sextus Placitus (fol. 76^r).

Later history: 14th-cent. press-mark and ex-libris of Bury St. Edmunds. Given by Sir Thomas Knyvett (d. 1544) to Augustine Styward. Presented to the Library in 1706 by Dr. Edward Tyson.

Bibl.: S.C. 2760g. Pächt & Alexander, iii, no. 53, pl. vi (fols. 32^r, 68^r, 89^r). Complete facsimile, ed. R.T. Gunther, The Herbal of Apuleius Barbarus..., Roxburghe Club 1925. Exh. cat., English illuminated manuscripts..., by J.J.G. Alexander & C.M. Kaufmann, Brussels 1973, no. 19, pls. 8a (fol. 10^v), 8b (fol. 76^r). E. Howald & H.E. Sigerist, eds., Corpus Medicorum Latinorum IV, Teubner, Leipzig 1927, p. XI.

MS. Bodley 130

123. Computistical and scientific miscellany.
c. 1110.

'The most important and the finest of the older English scientific mss.' (N.R. Ker). In spite of its date, the manuscript may perhaps be taken as a compendium of the learning of the pre-Conquest monasteries. Although very little of its contents can be described as classical, many ancient ideas are conveyed in its medieval texts,

by authors such as Bede, Helpericus and Abbo. The manuscript is notable for
its beautiful diagrams. That shown (fol. 7ᵛ), depicting 'sets of four', the elements,
the seasons, the four ages of man, etc., is an elaboration by Byrhtferth, monk
of Ramsey, of Bede, _De temporum ratione_, xxxv, and embodies the Platonic idea
of the harmony of the elements (_Timaeus_ 32B-C) which reached medieval
writers through sources such as Macrobius (_Comm._ I. vi, 23-40) or Isidore (_De
natura rerum_, VII. 4 and XI. 1-3, with diagrams).

    The volume was written probably at Thorney Abbey (Thorney annals were
soon added).

Later history: 16th-cent. marginalia by Robert Talbot. Given to St. John's College by Hugh Wicksteed at the beginning
    of the 17th cent. Borrowed by Robert Cotton, from whom it was recovered only after Laud's urgent entreaty of
    Nov. 1623. Five leaves (torn out between fols. 143 and 144) are still in the Cottonian collection.

Bibl.: Coxe, _College MSS._ For Byrhtferth's diagram, see C. & D. Singer in _B.Q.R._, 2 (1917), 47-51, fig. 3; C. W. Jones' edition
    of Bede's _D.T.R._ (The Mediaeval Academy of America. Publication No. 41), Cambridge (Mass.) 1943, pp. 368-9;
    R. W. Southern, _Mediaeval Humanism_, Oxford 1970, 164-5. For the history of the manuscript, see N. R. Ker in
    British Museum Quarterly, 12 (1937-8), 131-2. For miscellaneous entries in Old English, see N. R. Ker, _Catalogue of
    manuscripts containing Anglo-Saxon_, Oxford 1957, p. 435 no. 360.

               St. John's College, MS. 17 (+ London, Brit. Libr., Cotton Nero C. vii, fols. 80-84)

124. BOETHIUS, _De consolatione philosophiae_.

Second quarter of the 12th cent.

    In the miniature shown (fol. 1ᵛ. Front cover) Philosophy appears to Boethius
in prison. The figures on the right represent the Muses of poetry. The miniature
is the work of the artist of the Psalter from Shaftesbury (London, Brit. Libr.,
Lansdowne MS. 383), who is connected with Winchester and Hereford.

Later history: given by William Harwood, prebendary of Winchester, in 1611.   _Bibl._: S.C. 1856. Pächt & Alexander,
    iii, no. 103, pl. x (fol. 1ᵛ), with bibliography.   _MS. Auct. F. 6.5_   FRONT COVER

125. VEGETIUS, FRONTINUS, EUTROPIUS.

First half of the 12th cent.

One of the volumes written under the direction of William of Malmesbury (c. 1090 – 1143), who prefixed two elegiac couplets in his own hand (fol. 3ʳ):

'His sua Willelmus detriuit tempora libris,

Coniungens studiis haec quoque parua suis.

Quos animi causa poteris percurrere lector,

Nam cum summa grauant, inferiora iuuant.'.

Eutropius was also included in William's larger miscellany on ancient history, MS. Arch. Seld. B. 16. The two volumes show his concern to seek out and put together related texts.

A 15th-cent. inscription (a slip pasted on fol. 3ʳ) records that the manuscript was given to Lincoln College by Robert Flemmyng, who wrote a marginal note on fol. 85ᵛ.   Page exhibited: fol. 9ʳ, end of Vegetius, Bk. I; beginning of chapter-headings to Bk. II.

Bibl.: Coxe, College Mss. N. R. Ker in English Historical Review, 59 (1944), 371-6, esp. 375, and fig. 3 (fol. 3ʳ). H. Farmer

in Journal of Ecclesiastical History, 13 (1962), 46-7.

Lincoln College, MS. 100   PLATE XXI

126. ROBERT of Cricklade, De connubio patriarchae Iacob.

Second half of the 12th cent.

Robert of Cricklade was a canon of Cirencester when he wrote this work, c. 1138. We show it for the quotations (e.g. on fol. 126ᵛ, shown) which its author introduced from the second half of Seneca's Letters. The Letters were in circulation up to the late 13th cent. in two halves (1-88, 89-124). The S.W. Midlands was the one part of Europe in the first half of the 12th cent. where the two halves were read. A manuscript from Gloucester containing both halves is now London, Brit. Libr., MS. Harl. 2629, and quotations from both halves are found in William of Malmesbury's <u>Polyhistor</u>.

This English manuscript contains a 12th-cent. <u>ex-libris</u> of Reading Abbey.

<u>Later history</u>: acquired by Laud in 1638.   <u>Bibl.</u>: Coxe, <u>Laudian manuscripts</u>, cols. 1516-17. Pächt

&c Alexander, iii, no. 207. L.D. Reynolds, <u>The medieval tradition of Seneca's Letters</u>, Oxford 1965, 117, 120, 122-3.

<u>MS. Laud Misc. 725</u>

127. TERENCE.   Middle of the 12th cent.

The miniatures in this manuscript descended from their classical original through a Carolingian manuscript, Paris lat. 7899, of which this is probably a direct copy, though with some changes introduced from another source. Our miniatures are by four hands of whom one (e.g. on fol. 4ᵛ, exhibited, illustrating <u>Andria</u>, Act I, Sc. 1) is identifiable as W. Oakeshott's 'Master of the Apocrypha Drawings' in the Winchester Bible. It is still to be explained how exactly an English 12th-cent. copy came to be made of a 9th-cent. manuscript written in France and bearing (fol. 41ʳ) a 13th-cent. <u>ex-libris</u> of St.-Denis. Oakeshott discusses the relationship between these 12th-cent. miniatures and their classical originals: 'The loose classical folds are replaced by the elaborate formal patterns of the twelfth century. The mask has become something grim and terrifying. In these two books two worlds are in direct touch, but the later grotesquely misunderstands the earlier. So classical learning in the twelfth century was absorbed into a new synthesis which the Greeks and Romans would have found utterly incomprehensible.'

<u>Later history</u>: 13th-cent. <u>ex-libris</u> of St. Albans, fol. 1ʳ. Roger Walle, canon of Lichfield (<u>d</u>. 1488), fol. iiᵛ. Given by Frevile

Lambton of Hardwick, 1704. See <u>S.C.</u> for intervening owners.

<u>Bibl.</u>: S.C. 27603. Pächt &c Alexander, iii, no. 132, pl. xiv (fols. 2ᵛ, 47ʳ), with bibliography. L.W. Jones &c C.R. Morey, <u>The miniatures</u>

<u>of the manuscripts of Terence</u>..., Princeton etc. 1931, 68-93 and pls. (reproduces all the miniatures). W. Oakeshott,

<u>The sequence of English medieval art</u>..., London 1950, 19, pl. 56 (fol. 4ᵛ).   <u>MS. Auct. F. 2.13</u>

128–140. England & France,
12th to 14th centuries.

For the period in England and France from the 12th to the 14th centuries, the manuscripts chosen provide a good representation of the kind of books in which Latin classical texts were used and studied, from splendid large volumes to the working copies of individual scholars. This section also illustrates the way in which certain texts, notably Seneca's Tragedies and Dialogues, which were not in circulation in the Carolingian period, made their appearance (nos. 134, 140).

128. MARTIANUS CAPELLA, with commentary of Remigius of Auxerre.
Middle of the 12th cent.

A de-luxe copy, written in England, in a large format with the text in long lines and the margins ruled for the commentary. Several quires are missing after fol. 32, with the text of II. 175 – VI. 632. The commentary is the B version of Remigius, i.e. in the full form only for the first books (breaking off here at II. 71. 13, Lutz's edition p. 193 line 1, because of the missing leaves).

The manuscript later belonged to a notable book-collector, Nicholas of Sandwich (an Oxford M.A. by 1305), who gave it to his protégé Master William Rede, fellow of Merton and later bishop of Chichester (d. 1385). It is the first book listed in the indenture by which Rede made his magnificent benefaction of 1374 (?) to Merton.

Bibl.: Coxe, College MSS. C. Leonardi in Aevum, 34 (1960), 425-6. C.E. Lutz in Catalogus translationum et commentariorum (ed. P.O. Kristeller), II, Washington 1971, 373 (but the commentary does not end in Bk. I at fol. 12 as she states there). F.M. Powicke, The medieval books of Merton College, Oxford 1931, p. 168 no. 539. For Nicholas of Sandwich and Rede see A.B. Emden, A biographical register of the University of Oxford to A.D. 1500, III, Oxford 1959, 1639-40, 1556-60. Pages exhibited: fols. 10ᵛ-11ʳ.

Merton College, MS. 291

129. CICERO, Philippics; etc.   Second quarter of the 12th cent.

Written probably in France. Closely related to Leiden, Voss. Lat. O. 2 (Clark's n), and of some textual importance, especially for XIII. 29 to the end, where n is lost.

Later history : given by William Say (see no. 153).

Bibl.: Coxe, College MSS. This manuscript is o in A.C. Clark's ed., Orationes II, O.C.T. 1901. See also Clark in Classical Review, 14 (1900), 45–6, 250–1.

New College, MS. 252

130. CICERO, De officiis, De natura deorum, with part of De divinatione as Bk. IV, Philippics I–III, and part of IV.

Second half of the 12th cent.

For the De natura deorum the manuscript is a descendant of Vienna lat. 189 (now defective), and is cited as O by editors where that MS. fails. The manuscript is probably English, and there is a list of contents on the front flyleaf in an English hand of c. 1200. Annotations and additions in a cursive hand, apparently English, early 14th-cent., include on the last leaf (fol. 100^v) a list of the members of the household of an unidentified ecclesiastical dignitary. Some of the names are French and Italian (for a transcript, see Appendix).

The manuscript is now bound up with a 13th-cent. manuscript of Palladius.

Later history : sold by Thomas Trillek, bishop of Rochester 1364–72, to William Rede, who gave it to Merton.

Bibl.: Coxe, College MSS. Bibliography in the edition of De natura deorum by A. S. Pease, Cambridge (Mass.), 1955, i, p. 67.

Pages exhibited : fols. 62^v–63^r.   Merton College, MS. 311

131. CLAUDIAN, Opera.   (a) Late 12th cent. (b) c. 1200.

Two similar manuscripts of the same texts, bound together :

(a) Fols. 1–104. Works of Claudian only, written in England or France. It has fine illuminated and flourished initials, and though a small manuscript, is a de-luxe copy, probably intended for a well-to-do layman. According to Hall, the text of the De raptu Proserpinae at least, which belongs to the class with all lacunae, is closely related to Paris lat. 8082, which was owned by Petrarch. The glosses to the beginning of In Rufinum in our manuscript (fol. 15ʳ, exhibited) are identical to those on fol. 15ʳ of the Paris manuscript. The two copies are very similar in appearance.

(b) Fols. 105-272. Walter of Châtillon, Alexandreis, followed (fol. 169ʳ) by the works of Claudian. This manuscript is of similar type to (a), but slightly later. It too might have been written in England or France, to judge from both script and decoration (of the type sometimes described as 'Channel School'). The decoration is of even finer quality than (a)'s, and the parchment is very thin and well prepared.

Later history : see S.C. Presented by Thomas James, Bodley's first librarian, in 1601.

Bibl. : S.C. 2077. Pächt & Alexander, iii, nos. 248, pl. xxiv (fol. 15ʳ), and 299, pl. xxvi (fol. 202ᵛ). For the text see J.B.

Hall's edition of De raptu Proserpinae, Cambridge 1969, 19, 57 n.1 ; M.C. Colkes in Harvard Studies in Classical

Philology, 61 (1953), 162-4 (our MS. is 'probably the most accurately copied' of the early Mss.). For Paris lat. 8082,

see É. Pellegrin in Italia medioevale e umanistica, 7 (1964), p.504 and in La bibliothèque des Visconti et des Sforza.

Supplément, 1969, p.3 and pl. 15 (fol. 15ʳ), where it is described as French, 13th-cent.; L. Chiovenda in Archivum

Romanicum, 17 (1933), pl. 28.   MS. Auct. F. 2.16

132. PLINY, Natural History, Bks. I-XIX.   Early 13th cent.

Pliny's Natural History (or parts of it) was known to Bede and Aldhelm, and the remains of a manuscript written in Northumberland in the 8th cent. survives at Leiden (Voss. Lat. F. 4 = C.L.A. x, no. 1578). Whether Pliny survived the Viking invasions is not established.

J.G. Milne claimed that the present manuscript is closely related to London, Brit. Libr., Arundel 98 (12th-cent., English) and that both represent the type of text from which Robert of Cricklade (see no. 126) made his excerpts in the

12th cent. Another closely related 12th-cent. manuscript, probably English, is Le Mans 263. E. de Saint-Denis remarked of this group of manuscripts (which also includes Leiden, Voss. Lat. F.42, 14th-cent.): '…ils nous permettent de retrouver plus sûrement une tradition remontant à l'*ordo uetustiorum*'.

Our manuscript has the early 13th-cent. ex-libris of St. Albans Abbey, erased, and was later given (back) to the Abbey by the bibliophile Richard de Bury, bishop of Durham (d. 1345). In the 15th cent. it was pledged between 1453 and 1462 in the Queen's chest of Oxford University, jointly, by Dom John Warder, monk of St. Albans, and by the Carmelite Master, Johannes Consobrinus (or Portigall). It was pledged again, in 1467, in the Chichele chest by Robert Woodstock. In March 1471/2 the book was bought in London by John Russell, later bishop of Lincoln, who gave it to New College in 1482.

Page exhibited: fol. 9r, beginning of Bk. II, with fine initial.

Bibl.: Coxe, College MSS. For the history of the MS., see B.L.R. 3 (1950-1), 177-9. For the text, see especially J.G. Milne, 'The text of Pliny's Natural History preserved in English MSS.', Classical Review, 7 (1893), 451-2; E. de Saint-Denis, 'Un manuscrit de Pline l'Ancien ignoré des philologues', Revue de philologie, 3rd Ser., 34 (1960), 31-50 (on MS. Le Mans 263, with plates).

New College, MS. 274   PLATE XXII

133. Introduction to a commentary on CICERO, De amicitia.

Early 13th cent.

This is included as the earliest known example of a Latin classical piece written on paper. It is written in a hand that might be French or English, after a collection of medical and astronomical treatises.

Later history: bound up with several other manuscripts. From the collection of Christopher, 1st baron Hatton, purchased in 1671.

Bibl.: S.C. 4044. R.W. Hunt in Archives, 4 (1959-60), 49.   Pages shown: fols. 73v/75r (the small parchment slip, fol. 74, is an insertion to the preceding text).

MS. Hatton 112, fols. 58-78

134. Quotation from SENECA, Troades. Early 13th cent.

Seneca's Tragedies remained unknown on this side of the Alps until the third quarter of the 12th cent. From this time onwards, references begin to be found. The earliest full manuscript of the text in its northern manifestation was written in England in the first half of the 13th cent. (Cambridge, Corpus Christi College, MS. 406). This manuscript, an English copy of the Gloss (i.e. standard biblical apparatus) on Isaiah, contains a reference to one of Seneca's tragedies added by a contemporary hand. At Isaiah xxii. 13, 'Let us eat and drink, for tomorrow we shall die', the gloss, taken from the Commentary of St. Jerome, ends with a reference to the view of Epicurus, 'After death there is nothing and death itself is nothing'. There is then a 'signe de renvoie', Æ. Θ., answered in the bottom margin by ƀΘ., which introduces Troades 394-406, headed 'Hanc sententiam Epicuri ponit Seneca in tragedia que Troas inscribitur his uerbis' (fol. 31ʳ, exhibited. Pl. XXIII).

The manuscript was given to New College by the founder, William of Wykeham.

Bibl. : Coxe, College MSS. For the Cambridge MS., see R.H. Rouse, 'The "A" text of Seneca's tragedies in the thirteenth century', Revue d'histoire des textes, 1 (1971), 114. New College, MS. 21 PLATE XXIII

135. CICERO, Caesarian orations and Paradoxa. Early 13th cent.

Written probably in England. The Caesarian orations together with the Philippics (see nos. 129, 130) were the only group of Cicero's Speeches to enjoy some circulation in the High Middle Ages. In this manuscript the Caesarian orations are preceded by, among other texts, the Collatio Alexandri Magni cum Dindimo, a combination found in a volume bequeathed to the abbey of Bec by Philippe de Harcourt, bishop of Bayeux (d. 1163). On the front flyleaf is a contemporary list of contents with '145', and 'Z.18' added later. These pressmarks have not yet been identified:

fol. iiiʳ

Later history : Thomas Brudenell (created Earl of Cardigan 1661) and his wife Mary Tresham. Bought by the Library in 1966.

Bibl.: Sotheby's catalogue 12 December 1966, lot 218.   Pages exhibited : fols. 55ᵛ–56ʳ.

MS. Lat. class. e. 48

136. SENECA, Opera.   End of the 12th or early 13th cent.

The volume contains all the genuine and spurious works of the younger Seneca, and includes the Controversiae of the Elder Seneca, who was not distinguished from the younger. The Naturales Quaestiones here shown do not survive in manuscripts earlier than the 12th cent., and their archetype had suffered damage. The present manuscript (J in Gercke's edition) belongs to the class which gives the books in the order IVb – VII, I – IVa. It was perhaps written in France, but had reached England by the late 13th cent.

Bibl.: Coxe, College MSS. Edition of the Naturales Quaestiones by A. Gercke, Teubner, Leipzig 1907. p. XXXIV.

Pages exhibited: flyleaf, verso, with table of contents, and fol. 1ʳ.

St. John's College, MS. 36

137. CICERO, Epistulae ad Familiares, excerpts from Bks. IX, X and XIII.
Second half of the 13th cent.

Written in France, probably at Paris. Included in a composite volume put together by William of Clare, who noted that he brought it with him when he entered the Abbey of St. Augustine, Canterbury, in 1277. The contents, which include the only known copy of the earlier statutes of the English Nation in the University of Paris (fol. 156), show that he had recently returned from there.

The text of the letters (fols. 37ᵛ col. I – 45ᵛ. I, line 2) consists of Bk. IX. 1 – 22 § 4, 24 §3–26 ; X 4–6, 9–12, 25–29 ; XIII 2–3, 12–15 § 1, 18–19 § 2. They are preceded by Cicero's De natura deorum and are followed without a break by a collection of letters of Gregory the Great.

Later history : Dr. John Dee (1527–1608) ; given to Corpus by Christopher Wase, fellow of the College.

Bibl.: Coxe, College MSS. For the text, see G. Kirner in Studi italiani di filologia classica, 9 (1901), 387–8. For Dee, see

   M.R. James, Manuscripts formerly owned by John Dee (Transactions of the Bibliographical Society, Suppl. no. 1), 1921, p. 29.

Pages exhibited : fols. 37ᵛ–38ʳ.   Corpus Christi College, MS. 283   PLATE XXIV

138. Florilegium, including extracts from TIBULLUS and VALERIUS FLACCUS.   First half of the 13th cent.

Collections of extracts became common in the 12th cent., and included extracts from authors not in general circulation, such as Valerius Flaccus and Tibullus (see fol. 37ʳ, exhibited). The florilegium shown here was written in France and is independent of the more widely circulating Florilegium Gallicum.

Later history : on fol. 1ʳ is 'Cardigan', 17th-cent. A similar note is in no. 135, which belonged to Thomas Brudenell, created earl of Cardigan in 1661.

Bibl. : S.C. 29224. B. L. Ullman, 'Classical authors in mediaeval florilegia', Classical Philology, 23 (1928), 163–9.

   Valerius Flaccus, Argonauticon, ed. E. Courtney, Teubner, Leipzig 1970, xxxi.   MS. Add. A. 208

139. MAXIMIANUS, Elegies; STATIUS, Achilleis; CLAUDIAN, De raptu Proserpinae.   13th cent.

A school book, probably written in France. The Elegies of Maximianus are followed (fol. 10ʳ, exhibited) by the beginning of one of the anonymous poems found in the same position in no. 105.   Later history: Soranzo (typical foliation) → Canonici (?) →

   W. Sneyd. H. W. Garrod. Bought in 1961.   Bibl. : see no. 105.   MS. Lat. class. e. 47

140. SENECA, Dialogues.   14th cent.

The Dialogues only began to circulate outside Italy in the first half of the 13th cent., and were rare enough to be 'discovered' by Roger Bacon, who sent extensive extracts to Pope Clement IV. The manuscript shown, which is written in a hand more like that used for liturgical books, has 'a certain degree of affinity' with the text used by Bacon.

Given to Balliol College by William Gray, bishop. of Ely (d. 1478). The 15th-cent. annotations (see fols. 41ᵛ– 42ʳ, exhibited) are in the hand of Gray's friend Richard Bole. *Bibl.*: R. A. B. Mynors, *Catalogue of the manuscripts of Balliol College*, Oxford 1963, 107-8. For the text, see L. D. Reynolds in *Classical Quarterly*, N. S. 18 (1968), 371. For Bole's hand, see Exh. Duke Humfrey 1970, p. 25.

Balliol College, MS. 129

141-151. Italian Humanism

It is extraordinary that we should be able to illustrate this period by a series of such distinguished examples: classical manuscripts worked on by Petrarch, Coluccio Salutati, Niccolò Niccoli, Giovanni Aurispa, Piercandido Decembrio, cardinal Bessarion, Pietro Donato, Antonio Panormita, Bartolomeo Fonzio. In contrast, the section starts with a major classical manuscript written by a scribe who was no great scholar, but faithful to his exemplar.

141. CATULLUS.   14th cent., perhaps a little before 1375.

This manuscript ('O'), copied in Italy, is probably the earliest full text of Catullus to survive. It appears to be a faithful and literal copy of the exemplar, which, as O's mistakes suggest, is not likely to have been earlier than the mid or later 13th cent. A variant on fol. 21ʳ, exhibited, illustrates the point: at lxiv.11 the original text gives the nonsensical 'posteam', p̄ĉā, and a marginal note by the scribe reads 'proram', 'proā; it seems likely that 'proram' was the reading of the exemplar, and that O's scribe initially misread the second 'r' as 'e' because it was ligatured to the abbreviated 'p'; such a ligature ('biting') would be possible only in advanced gothic script. The other two 14th-cent. manuscripts read 'primam' and the accepted reading is 'prima'.

O throws no light on the origin of the exemplar. The rubrication was not completed at the time, but there are a few 14th-cent. cursive notes, apparently by the scribe, as on the page exhibited. The manuscript must have been in Lombardy around 1430, when an historiated initial was added on fol. 1ʳ in the style of the 'Master of the Vitae Imperatorum'.

Bibl.: Coxe, Canonici MSS. Pächt & Alexander, ii, no. 693, pl. LXVII (fol. 1ʳ), with bibliography. Facsimile, ed. R. A. B. Mynors (Codices Graeci et Latini phototypice depicti, XXI), Leiden 1966.

MS. Canon. Class. Lat. 30

142. SUETONIUS, Vitae XII Caesarum.   1351.

This manuscript was copied in Italy for Petrarch in 1351 and has marginal annotations made by him at various dates thereafter. On fol. 24ʳ, exhibited, is a note written by him at the very end of his life, where he uses the evidence of a Roman coin to supplement the account of the genealogy of the Caesars. Petrarch had recently been given this coin by his friend, the Augustinian friar Luigi Marsili, who was studying in Padua at this time.

Later history: Jean Grolier. Henry Drury. Bequeathed to Exeter College in 1895 by C.W. Boase, fellow of the college.

Bibl.: R. W. Hunt in The Times Literary Supplement, 23 Sept. 1960, p. 169. G. Billanovich in Italia medioevale e umanistica, 3 (1960),

28-57 and pls. V-VI. Bodleian Library exhibition, Fine bindings 1500-1700 from Oxford libraries, 1968 no. 9 (with

bibliography). A.C. de la Mare, The handwriting of the Italian humanists, I, i, 1973, p. 13 no. 19, pl. iii, f, h.   Exh. Ital.

Hum. 1974, no. 1.   Exeter College, MS. 186

143. PLINY, Nat. Hist., VI-XV.   Middle of the 12th cent.

Bks. VI-XXXVII survive from a copy of Pliny's Natural History which was written in the middle of the 12th cent., perhaps in the Mosan region. It was described by Campbell as being textually 'equal if not superior to those on which the text is now based.' By the late 14th cent. it had been bound in two volumes which were finally split up in about 1500. The Bodleian manuscript is the first volume, its beginning now lost, and the second, containing Bks. XVI-XXXVII, is now Paris lat. 6798.

While its two volumes were still together, the manuscript passed through the hands of several important humanists. It belonged to Coluccio Salutati (1331-1406) and to Leonardo Bruni (1370-1444), both chancellors of Florence, and bears notes in Salutati's hand. It was probably during Bruni's ownership that the manuscript was used by Niccolò Niccoli (c. 1364/5-1437). Niccoli himself owned and annotated a 10th-cent. copy of Pliny from Beauvais (now Florence, Ricc., MS. 488), which appears to have been the source for some of his emendations and additions of missing passages in Bruni's manuscript. More annotations were made by a subsequent owner, Antonio Panormita (1394 - 1471). The manuscript then passed to Ferdinand I, King of Naples, and can be identified as the 'codex regius' which Poliziano used in collating his printed text (see no. 150).

<u>Later history of the Bodleian part</u>: Clermont → Meerman.

<u>Bibl.</u>: <u>S.C.</u> 20621. Pächt & Alexander i, no. 275, pl. XIX (fol. 10ᵛ). Exh. Ital. Hum. 1974, no. 2. For the text, see D. J. Campbell

   in <u>American Journal of Philology</u>, 57 (1936), 120-3. For the later history of the MS., see R. W. Hunt in <u>Calligraphy</u>

   <u>and Palaeography</u>. Essays presented to <u>Alfred Fairbank on his 70th birthday</u>, ed. A. S. Osley, London 1965, 75-80

   (and see B. L. Ullman, <u>The humanism of Coluccio Salutati</u>, Padua 1963, 195-6, for the ex-libris in the Paris MS.).

   A. C. de la Mare, <u>The handwriting of the Italian humanists</u>, I, i, 1973, esp. pp. xvi, 42, 58, pl. XII (a), (b).

<u>MS. Auct. T. I. 27</u>

144. PROPERTIUS.   1421.

In this manuscript (formerly Holkham 333, L to the editors), the text of Propertius, lacking the first nine leaves, is accompanied by Petrarch's <u>Epistolae Metricae</u> (also imperfect) and the first 19 lines of the <u>Africa</u>. The whole manuscript was written in two columns in a fine cursive gothic bookhand by Johannes 'Campofregosa stirpe pia genitus', who signed and dated his work at the end of Propertius on fol. 17ʳ (see pl. XXV (a)). He is probably identifiable as Giovanni Fregoso or Campofregoso, brother of Tommaso Fregoso, the doge of Genoa, friend and patron of scholars, who was expelled from Genoa by Filippo Maria Visconti in Nov. 1421, only a few weeks after this colophon was written. Giovanni, who was in Genoa on 6 November 1421, followed his brother into exile at the Castle of Sarzanello, where Tommaso was visited and served by scholars such as Bartolomeo Guasco, who was in charge of his library when an inventory was made in 1425. The inventory was written at the back of Paris lat. 5690, a famous Livy which had earlier belonged to Petrarch.

In 1425 Tommaso owned a copy of the _Africa_, but there is no mention of Propertius or the _Epistolae metricae._ However, his possession of a manuscript from Petrarch's library may be important, since Giovanni's copy of Propertius belongs to the A family, and descends from Petrarch's lost manuscript, not through the copy made for Salutati, but through a lost sister manuscript. Our copy is also of significance because it has some readings which apparently derive from N (Wolfenbüttel, Gud. Lat. 224, _c._ 1200), the ancestor of the other Propertius family, and provides the earliest dated evidence of N's having been brought to _Italy_ (it may earlier have been at Metz, and was certainly in Rome in the 1460s).

Later history: bookplate of Thomas William Coke (1754-1842). Bibl.: text, see especially R. Postgate in _Transactions of the Cambridge Philological Society_, 4 (1894-9), 1-41, with plate; A. La Penna in _Studi italiani di filologia classica_, N.S. 25 (1951), 224-8 and passim. For Giovanni Fregoso, best known as a distinguished Genoese naval commander, see Litta, _Celebri famiglie italiane._ III, _Fregoso di Genova_, 1849, pl. III; C. Romano in _Arch. stor. lombardo_ XXIV (1897), 145; F.L. Mannucci in _Giorn. stor. della Lunigiana_, 5 (1913-14), 168 n.2. The inventory of Tommaso Fregoso was first printed by L. Delisle in _Cabinet des manuscrits_ II, Paris 1874, 346-7, and reprinted by Braggio in _Atti della Società ligure di storia patria_, 23 (1891), 281-2. N. Mann in _Italia medioevale e umanistica_, 18 (1975), pp. 503-4, no. 263. MS. Holkham misc. 36   PLATE XXV (a)

145. CICERO, Letters to Brutus, Quintus, Octavian (ps.-Cicero), Atticus.
First half of the 15th cent.

Written probably in north-east Italy (? Ferrara) by one careful humanistic hand, for the Sicilian humanist Giovanni Aurispa (1376-1459). The manuscript is on paper with a watermark of a triple mount, not in Briquet but nearest to his no. 11689. It is ruled with a hard point on the versos only, a method of ruling sometimes found at about this time in manuscripts written in north-east Italy. There is little or no original rubrication.

Up to fol. 108ᵛ the text belongs to the Σ family and has the same extensive omissions as MSS. Ravenna 469 and Vat. Pal. lat. 1510, both of the 15th cent. From this point on, it belongs to the Δ family, which descends from Salutati's manuscript, and is said to be related to Vat. Urb. lat. 322, a Florentine manuscript of about 1470. Our manuscript has received little attention even from recent editors, but considering its provenance, it would almost certainly repay closer study. It is quite likely to be the earliest of its group.

In the first part, up to fol. 72^r, and in fols. 106^v-8^r, Aurispa himself corrected and annotated the manuscript quite carefully, adding the headings and the Greek in the spaces left by the scribe (see pl. XXV (b)). His corrections are partly of simple errors and omissions by the scribe, and partly appear to be conjectures, but some derive from a manuscript of the Δ family — e.g. the correction 'tecum' for 'tectum' on fol. 71^v, exhibited (ad Att. II.5, § 1; Watt's edition, p.55 line 3). The second part of the manuscript was copied by the same scribe, but possibly after an interval, and Aurispa may not have bothered to correct it or to have the rubrication completed because he had found a better complete text. In August 1447 he wrote to Panormita from Ferrara about a beautiful and unequalled manuscript which he owned by then: '...epistolae uero sunt completissimae et minus quam ullae corruptae; inueniri enim solent plerunque incompletae, emendatae uero munquam...'. Aurispa's annotations appear to be in his mature, rather than his early hand, so our manuscript may have been copied for him not long before this date.

On fol. 280^v is the ex-libris 'Hic est mei Iohannis liber Aurispe', and at the top of fol.1^r is 'xxx', written in the same ink as the text and perhaps an early pressmark. Later history: Henry White (his sale, Sotheby's 23 April 1902, lot 513). Bequeathed by C. M. Firth, 1931. Bibl.: Exh. Ital. Hum. 1974, no.8. For the text see W.S. Watt, ed., vols. II-III, O.C.T. 1958-65, especially vol. II.i, p.ix. He cites a few readings from our manuscript. Aurispa's letter to Panormita was edited by R. Sabbadini, Carteggio di Giovanni Aurispa (Fonti per la storia d'Italia),

Rome 1931, no. LXXXXI. Samples of Aurispa's script dated 1413 and 1455 are reproduced by him facing p. 3. The hand of Aurispa in MS. Vat. Ottob. lat. 1984, dated 1422, is reproduced by D. Fava in Accademie e biblioteche d'Italia, 6(1922-3), p. 115. Maestro Adriano Franceschini, who is preparing an edition of a very full inventory of Aurispa's books which he recently discovered, has kindly confirmed the attribution of the annotations to Aurispa.

MS. Lat. class. c. 7   PLATE XXV (b)

146. Notitia Dignitatum and other texts.   1436.

This manuscript contains not only a collection of texts relating to the defence of the late Roman Empire and its geography, including the Notitia Dignitatum, but also Dicuil's Liber de mensura orbis terrae, composed in 825. The whole collection is here given the general title 'Cosmographia Scoti' (fol. 1^r). Our manuscript was copied for Pietro Donato, bishop of Padua, in January 1436, while he was presiding over the Council of Basel. The exemplar was a 'vetustissimus codex' from the library of Speyer, as the note in Donato's hand records on fol. 170^r:

Exemplata ē hec Cosmographia que Scoti dicatur cum picturis ex uetustissimo Codice: quem habui ex Spirensi bibliotheca. Anno dni M·cccc·XXXVI. mense Ianuario. Dum ego Petrus donatus, dei pacentia episcopus paduanus, uice Sanctissimi dni Eugenij pape. iiij. Generali Basiliensi Concilio presiderem.

The annotations are also in Donato's hand (see pl. XXVI). Apart from a fragment of an early 10th-cent. manuscript from Speyer now at Maihingen (HS. I, 2, 2°. 37), this particular collection survives only in 15th-cent. copies, of which Donato's is one of the finest. It shows what may be achieved even at conferences.

The manuscript is written in a humanistic hand by a scribe who also copied a Terence at Basel in 1436, perhaps for Donato (Vat. Ottob. lat. 1368). The miniatures both here and in the Terence are by Perronet Lamy, an illuminator who worked for Amadeus VIII of Savoy, later elected Pope by the Council as Felix V, who was at that time in retirement at Thonon on Lake Geneva. The same scribe and illuminator prepared another copy of the collection, now Paris lat. 9661. Sabbadini suggested that the Paris copy was made for the Milanese humanist Piercandido Decembrio, who knew the text by 1437.

Our manuscript is identifiable as no 209, 'Cosmographie Scoti', in the inventory of Donato's books. Pages exhibited: fols. 146ʳ-7ʳ. Later history: Soranzo no. 30 in folio.

Bibl.: Coxe, Canonici MSS. Pächt & Alexander, i, no. 666, pl. LII (fols. 80ᵛ, 84ᵛ), and ii, no. 599, pl. LVI (fol. 67ʳ), with a very full bibliography. See also I.G. Maier in Latomus, 28 (1969), 960-1035, and J.J.G. Alexander's forthcoming article in the Proceedings of the Notitia Dignitatum conference held at Oxford in December 1974. For the entry in the inventory of Donato's books, see P. Sambin in Bollettino del Museo Civico di Padova, 48 (1959), 91. The scribe's colophon to Vat. Ottob. lat. 1368 is reproduced by J. Ruysschaert in Bibliofilia, 60 (1958), p. 339 fig. II. For the miniatures in Paris lat. 9661, see the facsimile, ed. H. O[mont], Notitia dignitatum imperii ..., Paris, n.d. **MS. Canon. Misc. 378**   PLATE XXVI

147. Origo gentis Romanae, De uiris illustribus, and AURELIUS VICTOR, De Caesaribus.   The 1450s.

This manuscript is bound up with another (fols. 2-84b) containing the translation of Xenophon's Memorabilia by cardinal Bessarion with a colophon dated 1453, apparently the date of the manuscript. The watermark of the paper in both manuscripts is scissors, close to Briquet no. 3668, which was in use in Rome in the later 1450s as well as elsewhere. Both belonged to Bessarion himself, and were probably written to his order. There is no decoration.

The second manuscript (fols. 85-156) is written in a humanistic hand still showing traces of gothic, perhaps by a non-Italian scribe. It was corrected by a different, distinctive, uneven, humanistic cursive hand (see fol. 123ʳ, exhibited). It seems possible that the scribe was a member of Bessarion's household. His hand recalls manuscripts written in Rome in the 1450s and 1460s.

It contains three texts: (fols. 85ʳ-123ᵛ) <u>Origo gentis Romanae</u>, followed by the <u>De uiris illustribus urbis Romae</u> often found attributed to the younger Pliny, and (fol.124ff.) Aurelius Victor, <u>De Caesaribus</u>. The three texts together are ascribed to Aurelius Victor in the heading on fol.85ʳ. Only one other manuscript, Brussels, Bibl. Royale 9755-63, is known to contain the <u>Origo</u> and the <u>De Caesaribus</u>, and these two manuscripts also contain 86 lives for the <u>De uiris</u>, instead of the usual 77. They derive from a common exemplar which probably originated north of the Alps and dated from after 1020 A.D. The Brussels manuscript is said to be of the latter part of the 15th cent. and to be written in a northern hand. It has two early <u>ex-libris</u>. One is of the 16th-cent. scholar Theodore Poelman (Pulmannus). The other reads: 'Liber Iohannis Loemel capellani ecclesie sancti Dionisii Leodiensis'. We do not know the date of this <u>ex-libris</u>, but if it is early a possible connection with the 'Johannes de Lumel' who wrote two manuscripts at Rome in 1459 and 1460 seems worth investigating. He is also identifiable as the second scribe of Venice, Marc., Lat. VI 60 (2591), a copy of Bessarion's <u>In calumniatorem Platonis</u> made for Bessarion himself. Indeed, it is conceivable that the cursive corrections here are in his hand.

The combined volume bears the autograph <u>ex-libris</u> of Bessarion on the front flyleaf and is identifiable as no. 239 in the list of his books given to San Marco in Venice in 1468 (cf. no. 85).

<u>Bibl.</u>: for bibliography on the text, see R. Gruendel's revision of F. Pichlmayr's edition <u>Sexti Aurelii Victoris liber de Caesaribus</u>..., Teubner, Leipzig 1970. On our manuscript, see especially A. Momigliano in <u>Athenaeum</u>, N.S. 36 (1958), 248-59. He quotes the opinion of F. Masai on the date and origin of the Brussels manuscript. For manuscripts signed by Johannes Lumel see J. Ruysschaert, 'Miniaturistes "romains" sous Pie II' in <u>Enea Silvio Piccolomini Papa Pio II (Atti del convegno per il quinto centenario</u>...), ed. D. Maffei, Siena 1968, p. 256 n. 61,

pl. 17. For the entry in Bessarion's inventory, see H. Omont in *Revue des Bibliothèques*, 4 (1894), 178. An edition

and study of Bessarion's inventories is being prepared by Dr. Lotte Labowsky. The Brussels manuscript is described

by P. Thomas, *Catalogue des MSS. de classiques latins de la Bibl. Royale de Bruxelles*, Ghent 1896, 87-9.

<u>MS. Canon. Class. Lat. 131, fols. 85-156</u>

148. CICERO, <u>De officiis</u>, etc.   1465

The earliest printed edition of any classical text, printed by Fust and Schoeffer at Mainz. This copy is on vellum, and its back flyleaf is a fragment from a 9th-cent. manuscript of Vergil (<u>Aen.</u> XI. 687-709, 712-735).

<u>Bibl.</u>: Hain no. 5238. Proctor no. 80.   <u>Later history</u>: given by Thomas Draper of All Souls.

(printed book) <u>Auct. L. 3. 6</u>

149. 'Codex Ashmolensis' (Fonzio's epigraphical collection).   End of the 15th cent.

The manuscript, a collection mainly of classical inscriptions and drawings of classical monuments, was put together by the Florentine humanist Bartolomeo Fonzio (<u>c.</u> 1446-1513). Earlier collections on which he drew include those of Ciriaco of Ancona, some of whose drawings of Greek antiquities only survive here in Fonzio's copies. Fonzio also collected material for himself, partly with the help of his patron Francesco Sassetti, the manager of the Medici bank. Some of the inscriptions from Lyons, which Saxl says appear for the first time in Fonzio's collection, were perhaps collected by Sassetti, who is known to have visited Lyons while he was with the Medici bank in Geneva. Fol. LV^v, exhibited, contains an inscription with a rubric which tells us that it was noted by Fonzio at Otricoli in Umbria when returning with Sassetti from a visit to Rome, probably in 1472.

<u>Later history</u>: bought by the Bodleian from Bernard Ashmole in 1964.

<u>Bibl.</u>: Pächt & Alexander, ii, no. 329, pl. xxx (fols. 63^v, 139^v). See especially F. Saxl in *Journal of the Warburg and Courtauld*

Institutes, 4 (1940-1), 19-46. Exh. Ital. Hum. 1974, no. 9. S. Caroti and S. Zamponi, *Lo scrittoio di Bartolomeo Fonzio* umanista fiorentino (*Documenti sulle arti del libro*, 10), Milan 1974, 84-90. A. C. de la Mare, 'The library of Francesco Sassetti' in *Studies presented to P. O. Kristeller*, Manchester 1975 (forthcoming).

<u>MS. Lat. misc. d. 85</u>

150. PLINY, <u>Natural History</u>.   1473; notes c. 1490.

The edition printed by Sweynheym and Pannartz at Rome in 1473, with a nearly contemporary copy of the collations of Politian (not in Politian's own hand). The manuscripts collated are designated by the letters 'a', 'b' and 'c', one of the earliest known instances of the use of letters of the alphabet as sigla. In a note at the end, dated 1490, Politian explained that 'a' and 'b' denoted two manuscripts in the library of San Marco in Florence (now Laur., Plut. 82, 1-2, and Ashb. 98 + Ricc., 488), and that 'c' was a manuscript in the possession of King Ferdinand I of Naples (part of it is now no. 143). Politian's note goes on to say that he gave private classes for the space of seven months to certain young Portuguese and Englishmen who had come to Florence to study. The Englishmen were Thomas Linacre and William Grocyn (see no. 87).

<u>Pages exhibited</u>: fols. 161ᵛ-162ʳ. Bk. XIII, 17-25.

<u>Bibl.</u>: J. M. S. Cotton in <u>Modern Language Review</u>, 32 (1937), 394-6. R. W. Hunt in <u>Calligraphy and Palaeography. Essays presented to Alfred Fairbank on his 70th birthday</u>, ed. A. S. Osley, London 1965, 78 and 79 n. 13. B. L. Ullman & P. A. Stadter, <u>The public library of Renaissance Florence</u> ... (<u>Medioevo e Umanesimo</u>, 10), Padua 1972, 216-7 nos. 791-3.

(printed book) <u>Auct. P. I. 2</u>

151. MARTIAL.   Third quarter of the 15th cent.

This manuscript is exhibited as an example of fine Renaissance calligraphy and in particular of the 'italic' script which was to be imitated in type by Aldus for his pocket editions of the classics (see no. 161). Its scribe is identifiable as the Paduan Bartolomeo Sanvito (1421 – 1511/12). It is written in his cursive hand. Sanvito started his career in Padua but moved to Rome at some point in the 1460s.

The manuscript could have been copied by him either in Padua or in Rome, since it appears to have been written quite early in his career (at present, manuscripts certainly attributed to him date from only about 1460), and he may have done the decoration himself. The rubrication, with its characteristic alternating colours, blue, red, green, purple (and gold in the headings) is certainly by his hand — in the fine capitals, for which he was famous. The frontispiece and initials appear to be quite early examples of the classicizing Paduan style sometimes called Paduan/Roman because of the difficulty of distinguishing the provenance. This style was first used at Padua in the late 1450s (cf. no. 154).

Fol. 1^r bears the arms of the Venetian Agnolo Fasolo, _b_. 1426, bishop of Cattaro 1457, Modon 1459, and Feltre 1464–1490. Fasolo had been a canon of Padua: from Feb. 1466 – July 1471 he is documented as a member of the Papal Curia, as secretary and referendary to Paul II. The manuscript is in a fine 15th-cent. binding, rebacked, of gold-tooled red morocco. De Marinis assigns this to the Veneto and points out the close similarity of the decoration to the binding of Naples, Bibl. Naz. IV. G. 65, Cicero, De officiis, with the Gonzaga arms. As it happens, that manuscript was also copied by Sanvito, perhaps for cardinal Francesco Gonzaga, probably rather later than our manuscript, and was decorated by the Master of the Vatican Homer, an artist of possible Paduan origins who was certainly working in Rome and for Gonzaga in the 1470s. The origin of the Oxford manuscript is therefore still uncertain. It should be pointed out, however, that it has drypoint rulings on the versos only, a peculiarity which is perhaps to be associated especially with manuscripts produced in north-east Italy.

Later history: on the green-stained front flyleaf (fol. i^v), in red, is 'Marini Nigri Liber' (16th-cent.?). Acquired _c_. 1622–3.

Bibl.: S.C. 2187. Pächt & Alexander, ii, no. 625, pl. Lx (fol. 1^r), with bibliography. On Sanvito, see in addition U. Meroni, Mostra

   dei codici gonzagheschi. Catalogo, Mantua 1966, passim (reproduces Naples IV G 65, pl. 133); P. Sambin in Italia

   medioevale e umanistica, 9 (1966), 273–4; J. Ruysschaert, 'Miniaturistes "romains" à Naples', Appendix to T. De Marinis,

La biblioteca napoletana dei re d'Aragona. Supplemento I, Verona 1969, passim ; A. Fairbank in Journal of the society for Italic Handwriting , 68 (Autumn 1971),7-9 ; Exhibition, Survie des classiques latins, Vatican 1973, section III by J. Ruysschaert, passim. For Agnolo Fasolo, see P. Paschini in Memorie storiche forogiuliesi , 39(1943 -51), 208-18 ; J. Ruysschaert in Scriptorium 8 (1954),101, and 'Miniaturistes ...', cit. supra, p. 269. For a comparison of the bindings of the Naples MS. and ours, see T. De Marinis, La legatura artistica in Italia, II, Florence 1960, nos. 1649, 1649 bis, with plates.

Page exhibited: fol. 131ʳ, beginning of Bk. X.   MS. Auct. F. 4. 33

152-155. Humanism outside Italy

We could not altogether omit a section on the spread of humanism to England (nos. 152-4), but we have deliberately restricted it because it was the subject of a recent Bodleian exhibition to itself. No. 155, a French manuscript with elaborate decoration, is written in a script showing strong Italian influence.

Exh. Cat., Duke Humfrey and English humanism in the fifteenth century, Bodleian Library Oxford, 1970.

152. PLINY the Younger, Letters.   c 1440 (before Feb. 1444).

Written in humanistic script, at the request of Duke Humfrey of Gloucester, by the Milanese humanist Piercandido Decembrio and decorated with initials in Milanese humanistic style. Decembrio organised the copying in Milan of a number of classical texts for Duke Humfrey. Our manuscript has Duke Humfrey's usual ex-libris at the end and is identifiable as one of the books that he gave to the University of Oxford in February 1444. It is the only manuscript given by Duke Humfrey to the University now in the Bodleian.

The text belongs to the eight-book family. At the end of Ep. V. 6 (fol. 55ʳ, exhibited), the end of the 'hundred-letter' text which was in circulation before

Guarino found a manuscript with eight books at Verona in 1419, Decembrio noted: 'Hucusque exemplar fuit satis emendatum'. In fact, as Sir Roger Mynors pointed out, the text of the manuscript up to this point is mixed and interpolated. Marginal notes of this sort are often not to be taken at their face value.

Bibl.: S.C. 2934. Pächt & Alexander, ii, no. 697, pl. LXVIII (fol. 12ᵛ). Exh. Duke Humfrey 1970, no. 12. Exh. Ital. Hum. 1974, no. 7.

For the text, see R.A.B. Mynors, ed., O.C.T. 1963, p. xiii n. 1.

<u>MS. Duke Humfrey d. 1</u>

153. Livy, Fourth Decade.   c. 1430-40.

Written in Florence in an Italian gothic hand showing some humanistic influence, and decorated with simple humanistic vine-stem initials. The text is one of only two 'pure' members of McDonald's ψ family of the Fourth Decade. All the members of this family are Florentine, and perhaps descend from a manuscript in Boccaccio's collection.

This Decade belongs to a set of Livy (New College, MSS. 277-9), of which the first volume bears the name of (William) Say, fellow of New College 1430 – 1443 and later dean of St. Paul's, d. 1468. He possibly acquired this set of Livy and a copy of Cicero, De oratore, Orator, etc. (New Coll., MS. 250) from a mysterious Englishman known at present only as 'Thomas S.', who wrote part of the Cicero and annotated it, and apparently also annotated the Livy (mainly the First Decade). Thomas S. seems to have been in Italy during at least the middle of the 15th cent.

Bibl.: Coxe, College MSS. For the text, see A.H. McDonald, ed., O.C.T. Livy vol. 5, 1965, pp. xv-xvii. For the provenance of this set of Livy see A.C. de la Mare, 'Florentine manuscripts of Livy in the fifteenth century' in Livy, ed. T.A. Dorey, London 1971, 177-9. For Say and Thomas S., see Exh. Duke Humfrey 1970, nos. 32-3, 54-9 and pp. 15, 32.

Pages exhibited: fols. 23ᵛ-24ʳ.

<u>New College, MS. 279</u>

154. LUCRETIUS, De rerum natura.   c. 1460.

Written at Padua for John Tiptoft, earl of Worcester, who was studying there from c. 1459-61. Tiptoft's arms are on fol. 4ʳ (exhibited). The classical plinth with the inscription 'AETERNUM·FELIX' in which they are set, supported by two putti, holding scrolls with the motto 'AD ASTRA TENDIMUS', is an early example of the Paduan classical style of decoration. The scribe, who signs himself 'V.f.I.' (fol. 122ᵛ) writes a rather odd, distinctive, humanistic hand. He may have been a Northerner, perhaps an Englishman; but he seems to have worked mainly in Padua. Other manuscripts or parts of manuscripts copied by him have been identified, several of which were owned by 15th-cent. English collectors, including probably Tiptoft himself, and one must have been copied in England. One annotation in the manuscript, a pointing hand, is attributable to Tiptoft (fol. 4ᵛ). His manuscript is the first known copy of Lucretius to be brought to England.

Later history : given by Jane Owen in 1610.   Bibl.: S.C. 3045. Pächt & Alexander, ii, no. 606, pl. LVIII

(fol. 4ʳ). Exh. Duke Humfrey 1970, no. 72 and pp. 41-2. G. Mariani Canova, La miniatura veneta del Rinascimento

1450 - 1500, Venice 1969, p. 142 no. 7.   MS. Auct. F. I. 13

155. JUSTINUS, Epitoma Historiarum Philippicarum Pompei Trogi.   Third quarter of the 15th cent.

Copied and illuminated in France. The manuscript is written in a round gothic hand showing strong Italian influence, but similar to (though perhaps not identical with) the hand of Jean Derlons of Laon, master of the Collège de Laon in Paris, in Paris lat. 6958 (Simon of Genoa, Clauis sanationis), which he completed in Feb. 1471. The manuscript is illustrated with a series of miniatures which are of particular interest because only a few have been finished and the rest have been left at various stages of completion (e.g. fol. 85ʳ, exhibited). Manuscripts of classical texts, in French or Latin, with miniatures on a lavish scale, were not uncommon in 15th-cent. France.

The text is described by Ruehl as both contaminated and interpolated.

Later history : fols. 46ᵛ, 75ʳ, erased notes in a humanistic cursive hand of the late 15th or early 16th cent. On fol. 127ᵛ (flyleaf) is 'P.O.P.A.' (16th-cent.?) and on the front flyleaf (fol. Iᵛ) is a later armorial bookstamp, partly erased or rubbed and impossible to decipher.

Bibl.: S.C. 28025. Pächt & Alexander, i, no. 727, pl. LVII (fol. 57ᵛ). For the text, see F. Ruehl in Jahrbuch für Classische Philologie 6 (Suppl.) (1872), 84 no. 39. For Paris lat. 6958, see C. Samaran, R. Marichal, eds., Catalogue des manuscrits portant des indications de date, de lieu, ou de copiste, II, Paris 1962, p. 387 and pl. CXLVIII, where it is pointed out that Derlons also signed Le Mans MS. 242 (Avicenna), copied in Paris in 1462 and 1465.   MS. Auct. F. 2. 29

Post-medieval

156–159. Printers' copy, 16th-cent.

Manuscripts sent to a printer are often roughly handled, and it is not surprising that many copies of classical texts handed over to Renaissance printers did not survive; they were presumably thrown away as being of no further use. The result is that in certain cases the first printed text is of some importance for the modern editor because it represents a significant manuscript.

However, the copy used for many editions still exists and can be identified by the special marks added by the printers. Exhibits 156-7 show MS. C.C.C.97 and the edition of Proclus on Euclid which was produced from it by Hervagius at Basle in 1533. The point of division between pages 16 and 17 in the printed book is marked in red in the margin of fol.17ʳ in the manuscript: the note 6 B 17 refers to the sixth page of the second quire which is the seventeenth page of the whole book.

Exhibits 158-9 show a translation of Tacitus' Histories by sir Henry Savile, Warden of Merton College, printed in 1591. The manuscript is a copy made by a professional scribe, but Savile himself has added notes in the margin.

156-7. Corpus Christi College, MS.97   + (Bodl. printed book) Savile W.7.

158-9. MS. Eng. hist. d. 240   + (Bodl. printed book) 90 e. 3.

160-172. Classical scholars

Thanks mainly to Edward Bernard's purchases at Heinsius' sale in 1683 and to the D'Orville collection, Bodley is especially strong in printed classical texts which bear the annotations of famous scholars.

160. Erasmus (c. 1469-1536). His copy of the editio princeps of Euripides, Aldus, Venice 1503. The ex-libris is shown; there are no marginalia attributable to Erasmus in either volume.

Bibl.: N.G. Wilson in Antike und Abendland, 18 (1973), 87.   Lincoln College, s.n.

161. Antonio Seripandi (*d.* 1531). Cicero, *Epistulae ad familiares*, Aldus, Venice 1512. Note on back fly-leaf: 'has Ciceronis Epistolas Antonius Seripandus ex uetustissimo codice manuscripto emendauit, cuius manu quae ad marginem huius exemplaris uisuntur annotata sunt'. It is quite possible that the 'uetustissimus codex' was none other than the 9th-cent. manuscript now Florence, Laur., Plut. 49, 9, since a note by Seripandi on fol. 2ʳ speaks of the manuscript as belonging to the Medici cardinal. The work of annotation was done immediately before and after the sack of Rome in 1527. <u>MS. D'Orville 461</u>

162. Octauianus Ferrarius of Milan (1518–1586). Catullus, Tibullus, Propertius, Aldus, Venice 1515. There are extensive marginalia, especially in the Tibullus, where he cites readings from a manuscript. At the end of the Tibullus (fol. 76ᵛ) he gives a reading 'ex codice Romano uetustissimo'. Elsewhere he cites simply 'codex uetus', 'uetustus', 'ueterrimus', 'uetustissimus', 'antiquus', 'antiquissimus', etc. Such terms used by humanists are difficult to use in establishing the age of their manuscripts, but a manuscript described as 'antiquissimus' or 'uetustissimus' is unlikely to have been written much later than the 11th to 12th century, which is earlier than the oldest complete extant manuscript of Tibullus (Milan, Ambros., R 26 sup., 2nd half of the 14th cent.).

Lindsay published the variants of Ferrarius in 1898, but later editors of Tibullus do not seem to have taken them into account. It should be admitted that the readings do not appear to be very exciting.   Later history: N. Heinsius.

<u>Bibl.</u>: W. M. Lindsay in <u>Classical Review</u>, 12 (1898), 445–6. For the problem of dating humanists' references to manuscripts, see S. Rizzo, <u>Il lessico filologico degli umanisti</u> (<u>Sussidi eruditi</u>, 26) Rome 1973, 147–168.

<u>Auct. 2R. 6. 28</u>

163. Guillaume Budé (1467-1540). Pliny the Younger, letters. A volume made up of the edition of P. Beroaldus (1498) of Bks. I-IX and of the portion of Bk. X published by H. Avantius (1502), with the missing letters from books VIII and X supplied in manuscript by Budé. These supplements were derived from an 'exemplar uetustissimum' found by Giovanni Giocondo, of which a fragment is preserved in the Morgan Library in New York. Mynors showed that the manuscript was in the library of St. Victor at Paris.

Bibl.: facs. in E.A.Lowe & E.K.Rand, *A 6th-cent. fragment of the letters of Pliny the Younger*, 1922, pk XVII, XVIII. R.A.B. Mynors' edition, O.C.T. 1963, p. XVIII.   <u>Auct. L.4.3</u>

164. A. Turnebus (<u>d</u>. 1565). Plautus. Readings from the important lost 'codex Turnebi', the collations here being in the hand of Fr. Duaren (1509-1559).

Bibl.: W.M.Lindsay, *The codex Turnebi of Plautus*, Oxford 1898 (facsimile of this book).   <u>8° D 105 Linc.</u>

165-166. Scaliger (1540-1609). Many books from his library survive: shown here are his Plautus (title-page with inscriptions showing the book's later history) and Seneca's <u>Tragedies</u> (with collations from a v(etus) c(odex)).

<u>Auct.S.5.21</u> and <u>Auct.S.4.26</u>

167. Isaac Casaubon (1559-1614). His writing tablets. 'Notitias exhibent breues de itineribus suis, aliaque aduersaria parui momenti' (Coxe).

Bibl.: Coxe, <u>Greek MSS.</u>, col. 850.   <u>MS. Casaubon 61</u>

168. Isaac Vossius (1618-1689). His copy of Grotius' edition of Lucan, Leiden 1627, with notes and collations. He records scholia from one or more medieval manuscripts.   <u>Auct. S.4.16</u>

169-170. Nicholas Heinsius (1620-81). Two examples of his work as a collator of Ovid manuscripts. MS. Auct. F.4.25 is a 15th-cent. manuscript of the Fasti, Auct. S.5.8 an Elsevier of 1629 containing the Metamorphoses.

Bibl.: D.E.W. Wormell, Hermathena 93(1959), 38-62, esp. 47. M.D. Reeve in Rheinisches Museum 117(1974), 133-66, esp. 151. For MS. Auct. F.4.25, see S.C. 8864.

MS. Auct. F.4.25 ; Auct. S.5.8

171. Richard Bentley (1662-1742). His copy of Plautus, the Gronovius edition of 1669, where he made numerous corrections 'currente calamo'. P.564 shows him at work on a canticum in the Menaechmi.

Bibl.: E.A. Sonnenschein, Anecdota Oxoniensia, classical series I, pt. IV.   Auct. S. inf. I.27

172. Thomas Gaisford (1779-1855). Letter to Bandinel, Bodley's Librarian, about an offer to sell the Library some biblical manuscripts. The sum eventually paid was £373, not £800. The vendor Tischendorf is best known for the ingenuous means by which he obtained the codex Sinaiticus from the monastery of St. Catharine.

Bibl.: E. Craster, History of the Bodleian Library 1845-1945, Oxford 1952, 87.

MS. Don. d. 145, fol. 214

Concordance of shelfmarks

References are to item numbers

Bodleian manuscripts

MSS. Add. A. 208 (138), C. 136 (26), C. 144 (94).

MSS. Auct. E. 4. 12 (66).

F. 1. 13 (154), 15, fols. 78-92 (118), 16 (24).

2. 8 (23), 13 (127), 14 (120), 16 (131), 20 (121), 29 (155).

3. 24 (63).

4. 25 (169), 32 (117), 33 (151).

5. 25 (97).

6. 5 (124), 23 (62), 27 (109).

T. 1. 24 (88), 26 (90), 27 (143).

2. 7 (13), 8 (67), 11 (77), 19 (101), 20 (102), 26 (34), 27 (106), 28 (104).

4. 7 (83), 13 (61).

V. 1. 51 (12), 53 (73).

MS. Barlow 40 (116).

MSS. Barocci 6 (82), 24 (14), 50 (59), 116 (79), 120 (68), 131 (64), 133 (65), 182 (60), 217 (57).

MSS. Bodley 38 (105), 130 (122), 309 (93).

MSS. Canon. Class. Lat. 30 (141), 41 (113), 50 (112), 54 (27), 131 (147), 279 (103).

MSS. Canon. Gr. 11 (80), 26 (81), 43 (20), 65 (75), 79 (19), 87 (86), 93 (72).

MS. Canon. Misc. 378 (146).

MS. Canon. Pat. Lat. 175 (115).

MS. Casaubon 61 (167).

MS. E. D. Clarke 39 (56).

MS. Don. d. 145, fol. 214 (172).

MSS. D'Orville 77 (107), 95 (107), 158 (110), 301 (55), 461 (161).

MS. Duke Humfrey d. 1 (152).

MS. Eng. hist. d. 240 (158).

MSS. Gr. class. a. 1 (P) (3), 8 (P) (5), 10 (P) (41), 16 (P) (38).

b. 3 (P) (1), 19 (P) (42).

c. 72 (P) (44), 76 (P) (39), 77 (P) (37).

d. 22 (P) (35), 97 (P) (43), 114 (P) (40).

e. 21 (P) (8), 44 (P) (2).

f. 25-7 (P) (30), 39 (P) (11), 41 (P) (10), 75 (P) (4), 113 (P) (36), 114 (76), 124 (P) (33).

g. 7 (P) (7), 16 (P) (6), 49 (P) (9).

MS. Hatton 112, fols. 58-78 (133).

MSS. Holkham Gr. 83 (16), 84 (17), 88 (84), 112 (74).

MSS. Holkham Misc. 34 (91), 36 (144).

MS. Junius 25 (95).

MSS. Lat. class. e. 16 (P) (31), 20 (P) (50), 47 (139), 48 (135).

f. 5 (P) (49), 9-10 (P) (32).

g. 5 (P) (48).

MS. Lat. misc. d. 85 (149).

MSS. Laud Gr. 18(71), 54(70), 55(85).

MSS. Laud Lat. 29(99), 49(108), 104(96), 118(100).

MSS. Laud Misc. 130(98), 276(89), 725(126).

MSS. Rawl. G. 57(119), 111(119).

MS. Shelley e.4(29).

Bodleian printed books

90 e.3(159).

Auct. L.3.6(148), 4.3(163).

Q.1.2(150).

S.4.16(168), 26(166).

5.8(170), 21(165).

inf. I.27(171).

2R 6.28(162).

8° D 105 Linc.(164).

Savile W.7(157).

Oxford College Libraries

All Souls, MS. 82(25).

Balliol, MSS. 129(140), 275(92).

Christ Church, MS. Wake 5(58).

Corpus Christi, MSS. 97(156), 106(87), 108(54), 148(78), 283(137), 470(18).

Exeter College, MS. 186(142).

Lincoln College, MS. 100(125).

printed book (Euripides), s.n.(160).

Merton, MSS. 291(128), 311(130).

New, MSS. 21(134), 252(129), 258(69), 274(132), 279(153), 298(15).

Queen's, MS. 202(111).

St. John's, MSS. 17(123), 36(136).

Borrowings from outside Oxford

Egypt Exploration Society

P. Ant. 29(21), 30(22), 152(53).

P. Ant., s.n. (Juvenal), (51).

P. Oxy. 1814(52), 2088(46), 2103(47), 3208(45).

Eton College, MS. 150(114).

B.C.B.-B. scripsit calamo veloci. 6-17 Jul. 1975.

Plate I. No.15.

(a) Fol. 32ʳ (bottom half; reading downwards). Homer, _Iliad_ VI. 489–505, 528–9; VII. 1–13.

(b) Fol. 111ᵛ (detail; reading across). Johannes Tzetzes, _Allegoriae Iliadis_, I. 363–375; II. 1–16.

O ardani, delacrimas, ante oms pulcher iulus.

Atq; animu patriae strinxit pietatis imago;

Tum sic effatur;

Spondeo dignatus ingentib; oina coepit·

Namq; erit ista mihi genetrix nomenq; creuse

Solum defuerit; noe partum gratia tale

Paruaman & casus factum quicumq; sequitur

Caput hoc uroqg; pater ante solebat

Quae tibi pollice or redui rebus q; secundis

Haec eadem matriq; tuae generiq; manebu

Sic ait inlacrimans; humero simul exit ense

Auratu; miraqu fecerat arte lycaon

Gnosius; atq; habilem uagina aptarat eburna·

Da tniso mnestheus pelle horrentis q; leonis

Exuuias; galeam fidus permutat aletes·

Protinus armati incedut; quos omnis euntes

Primorum manus ad postas iuuenuq; senuq;

Prosequitur uotis; necnon & pulcher iulus

Anteannos animum q; gerens curamq; uirile

Multapatri mandata dabat postanda sedaure;

Oma discerpunt; & nubib; irrita donant;

Egressi superant fossas; noctisq; p umbram

Castra inimica p etunt; multis tam ante futuri

Exitio; passim somno uinoq; p herbam

Corpora fusa iacent; arrectos litore currus

Inter lora rotas q; uiros simul arma iacere

Uina simul prior hirtacides sic ore locutus

Euriale audendum dextra; nunc ipsa uoca res

Hac iter est; tu nequa manus se attollere nobis

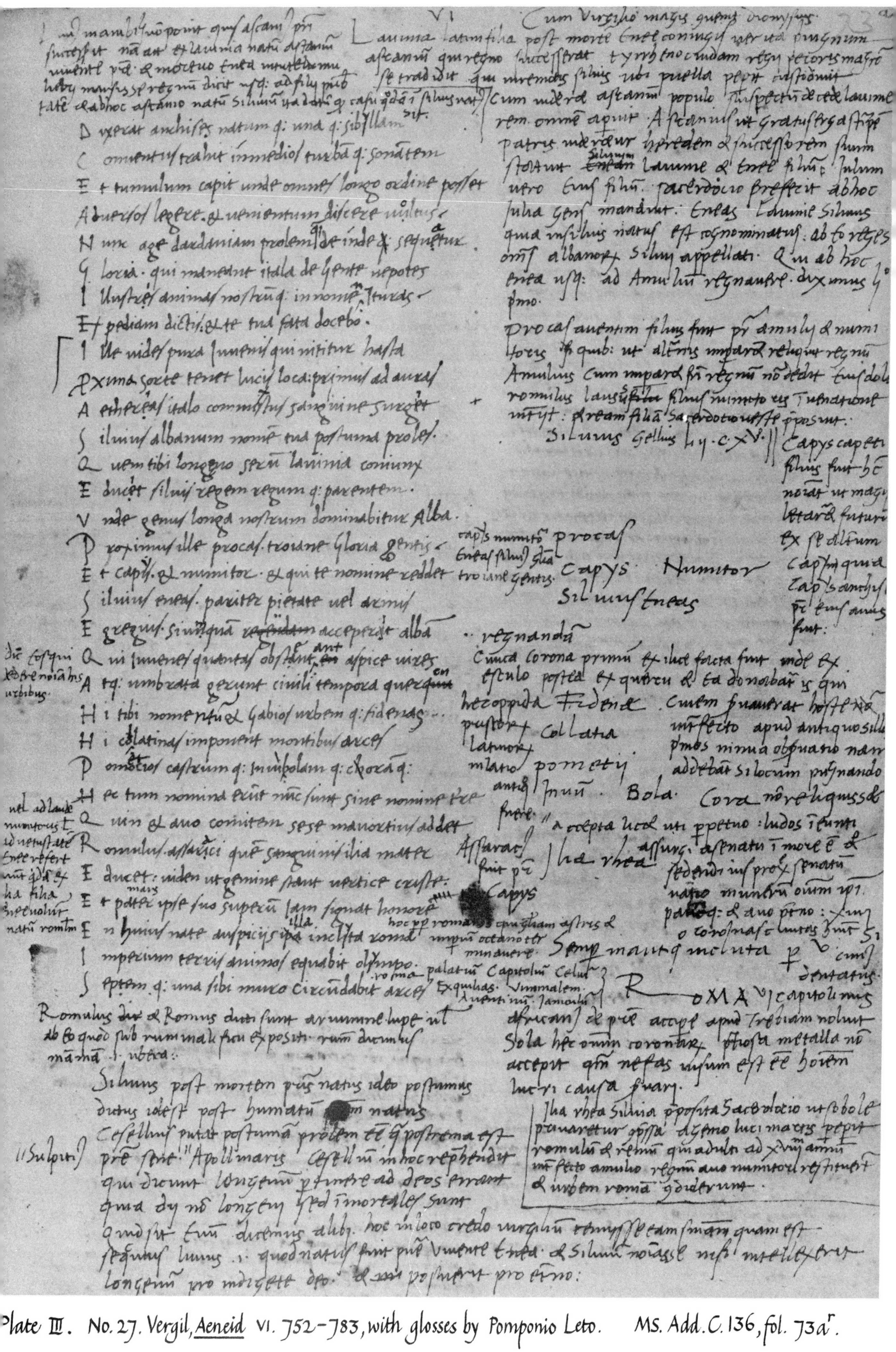

Dixerat anchises natum q: una q: sibillam
Conventus trahit in medios turba q: sonantem
Et tumulum capit unde omnes longo ordine posset
Adversos legere et venientum discere vultus.
Nunc age dardaniam prolem que deinde sequatur
Gloria. qui maneant itala de gente nepotes
Illustres animas nostrumq: in nomen ituras.
Expediam dictis et te tua fata docebo.
Ille vides pura iuvenis qui nititur hasta
Proxima sorte tenet lucis loca: primus ad auras
Aethereas italo commixtus sanguine surget
Silvius albanum nomen tua postuma proles
Quem tibi longevo serum lavinia coniunx
Educet silvis regem regum q: parentem.
Unde genus longa nostrum dominabitur Alba.
Proximus ille procas troiane gloria gentis
Et capys et numitor et qui te nomine reddet
Silvius eneas. pariter pietate vel armis
Egregius si umquam regnandam acceperit alba
Qui iuvenes quantas ostentant aspice vires
Atq: umbrata gerunt civili tempora quercu
Hi tibi nomentum et Gabios urbem q: fidenas
Hi collatinas imponent montibus arces
Pometios castrum q: inui bolam q: coram q:
Hec tum nomina erunt nunc sunt sine nomine terrae
Quin et avo comitem sese mavortius addet
Romulus assaraci quem sanguinis ilia mater
Educet: viden ut geminae stant vertice cristae.
Et pater ipse suo superum iam signat honore
En huius nate auspiciis illa incluta roma
Imperium terris animos equabit olympo.
Septem q: una sibi muro circumdabit arces

Plate III. No. 27. Vergil, <u>Aeneid</u> VI. 752–783, with glosses by Pomponio Leto. MS. Add. C. 136, fol. 73a^r.

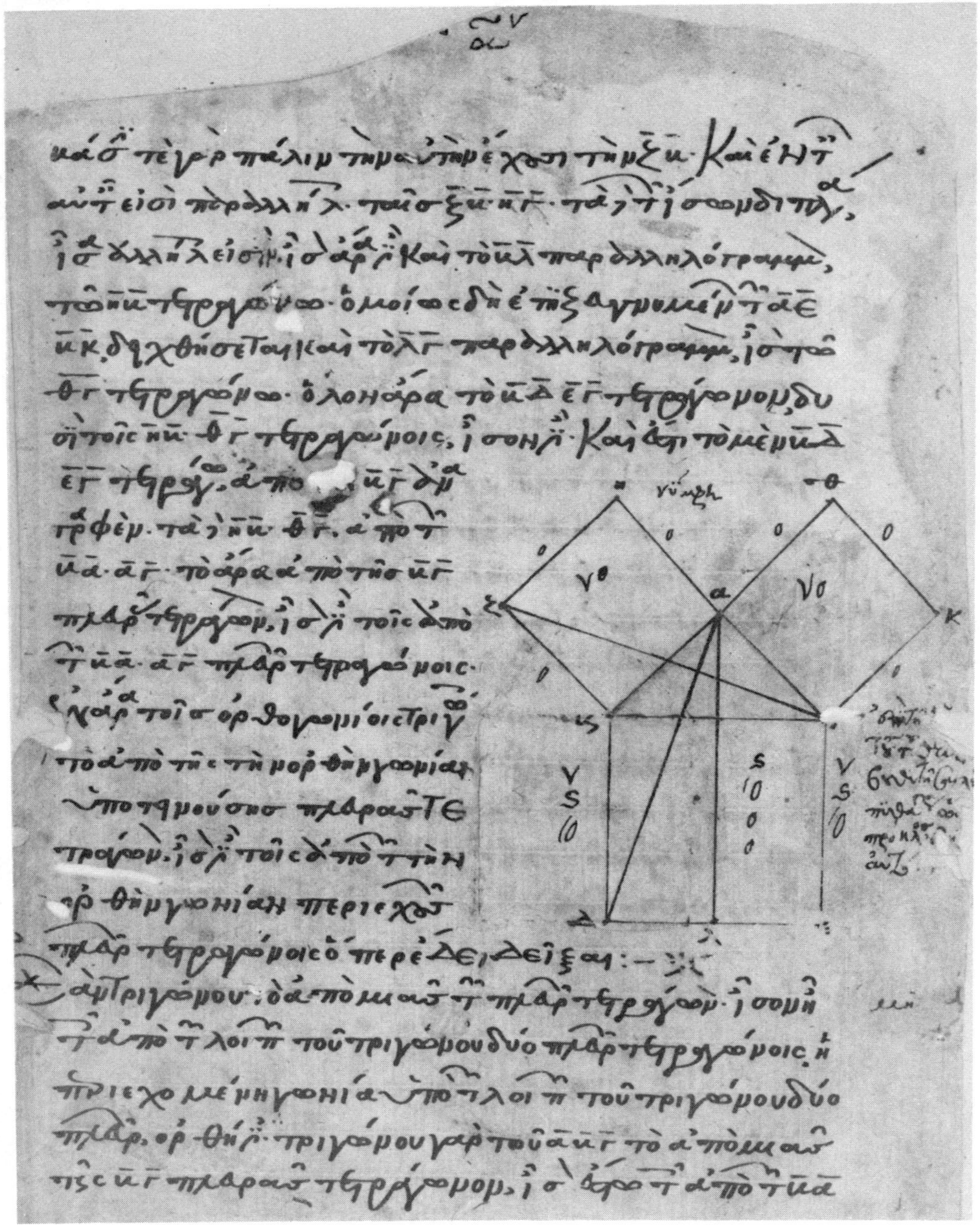

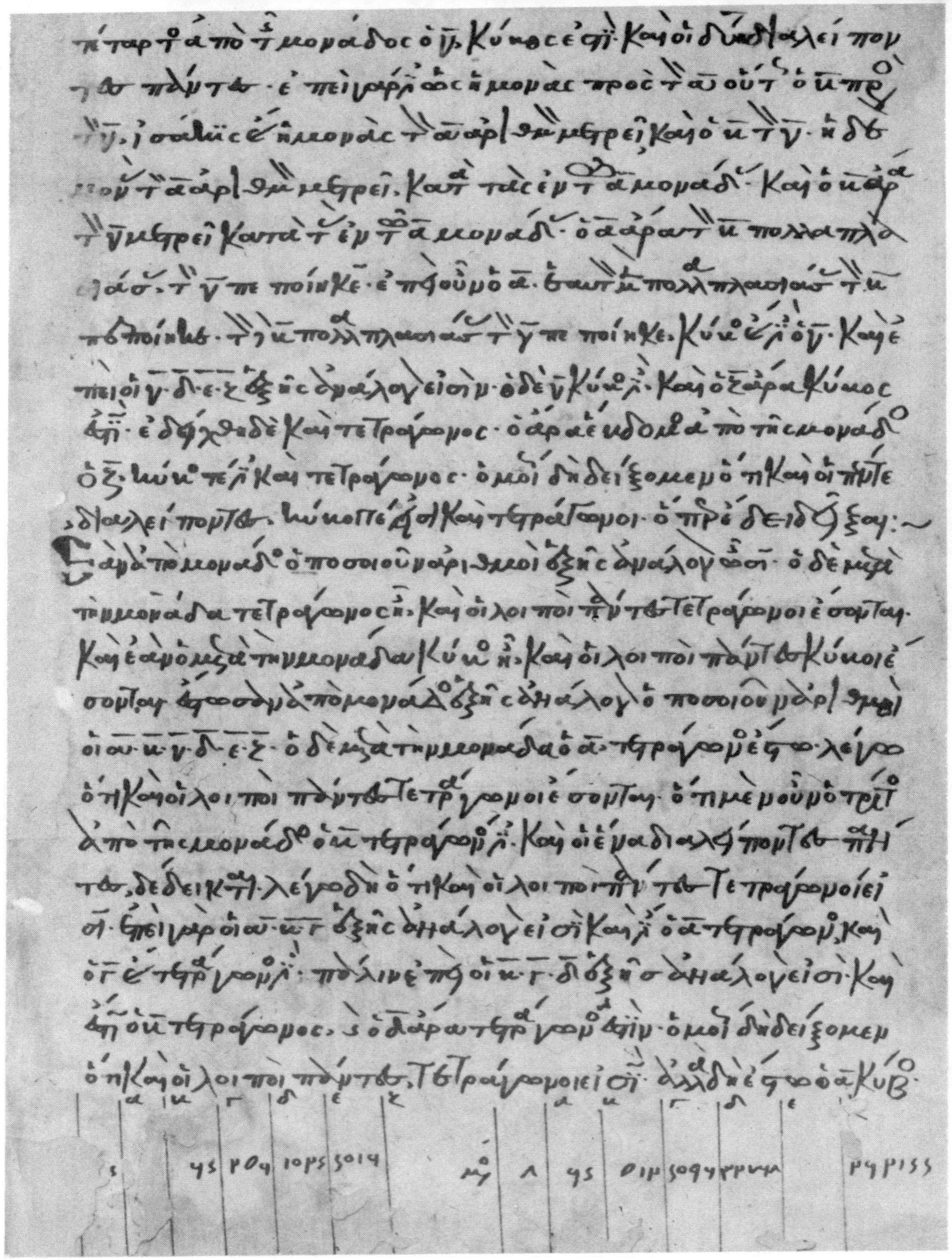

Plate IV. No. 62. Euclid, Elements. MS. Auct. F. 6. 23. (a) Fol. 15ʳ. Bk. I. 47 (Pythagoras' theorem) — 48. (b). Fol. 127ʳ. Bk. IX. 8–9.

ὑπόθεσις τ(οῦ) κατὰ λεωκράτους·

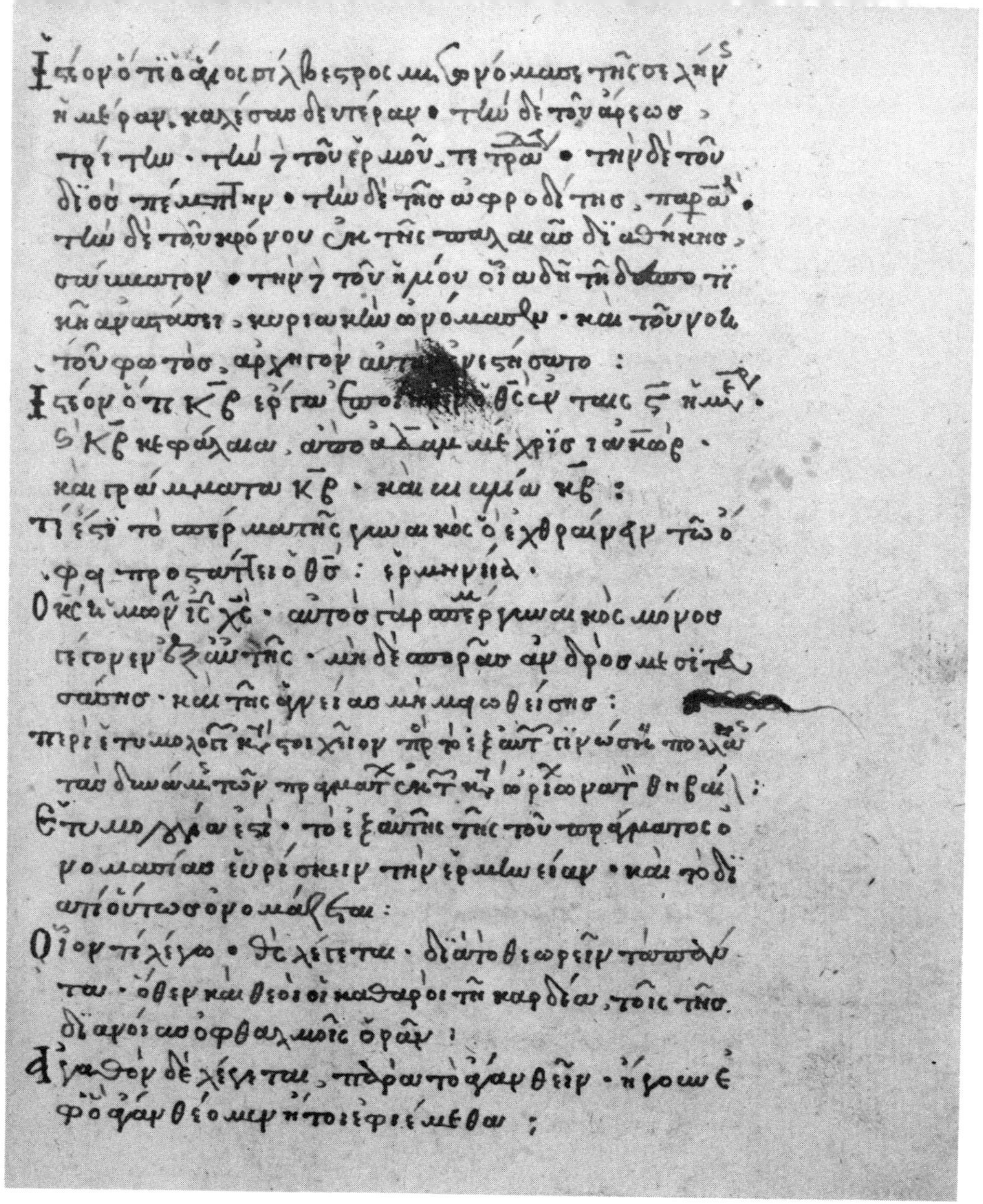

Plate VII (a). No. 77. Orion, Etymological dictionary (abridgment).
MS. Auct. T. 2. 11, fol. 323ʳ.

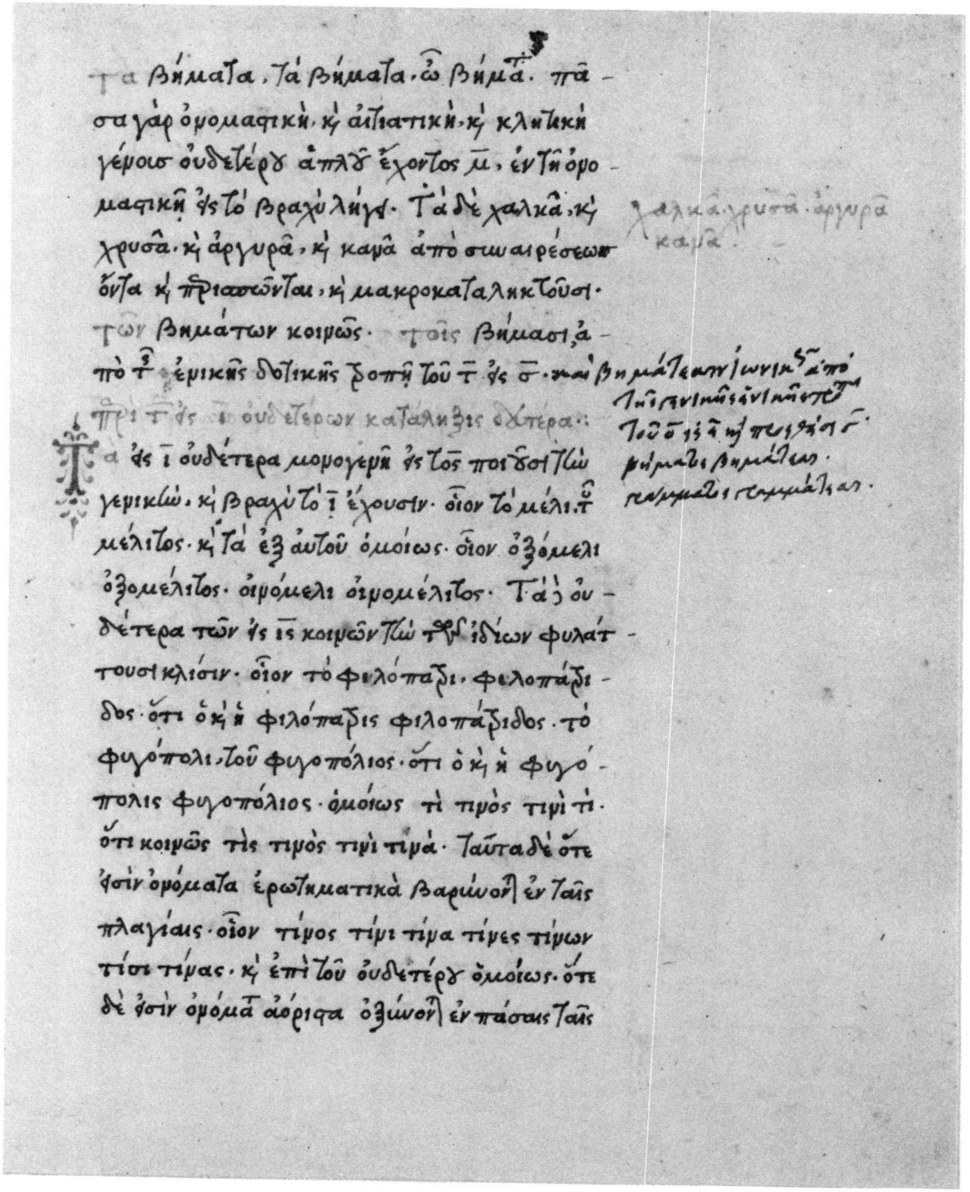

Plate VII (b). No. 82. Constantine Lascaris. MS. Auct. T. 4. 7, fol. 151ʳ.

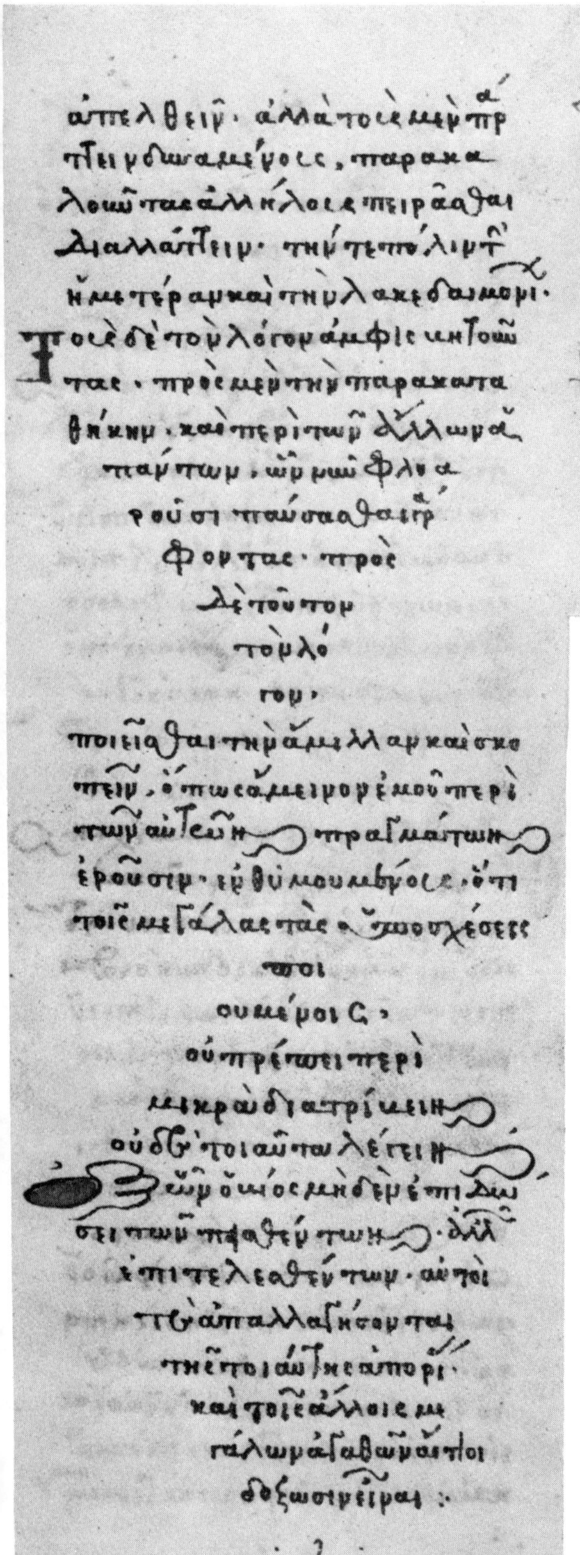

Plate VIII (a). MS. Canon. Gr. 87, fol. 119ᵛ.
No. 86. Isocrates, Panegyricus, 188–9 (end), with cryptographic colophon.

Plate VIII (b). MS. Gr. class. f. 114, fol. 171ᵛ.
No. 76. (i) Λέξεις τῶν ἐπῶν τοῦ ἁγίου Γρηγορίου τοῦ Θεολόγου (end).

(ii) John Philoponos, περὶ τῶν διαφόρων σημασιῶν διαφόρως τονουμένων (start)

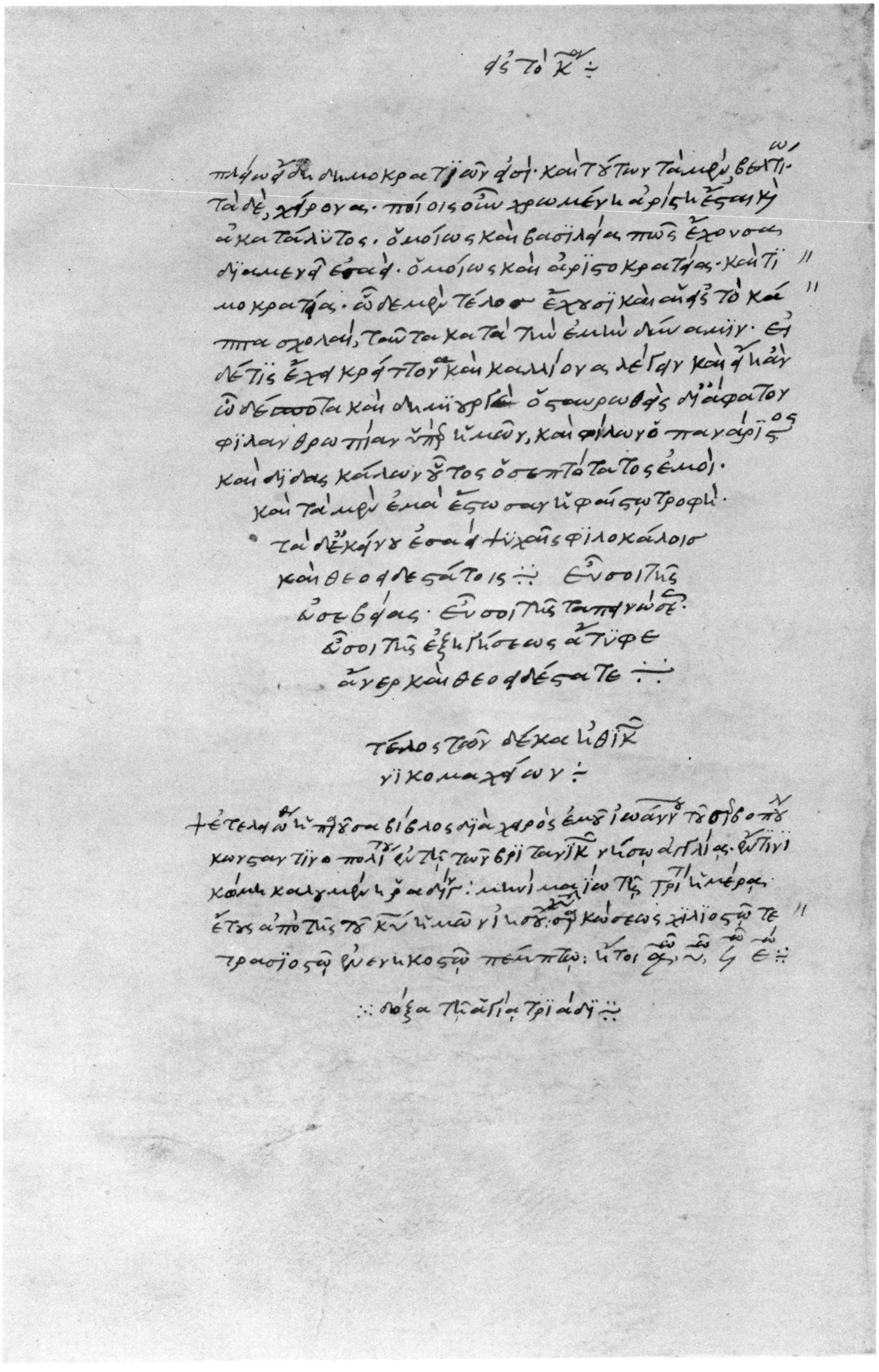

primo per publicum ductq. nunc priuata passim subeant uecta. formaq.
urbis fit occupatq. magis quã diuisis similis.
TITI LIVII NICOMACHVS. DEXTERVM EMENDAVI
AD EXEMPLV PARENTIS MEI CLEMENTIANI AB VRBECONS
VICTORIANVS EMENDABAM. DOMNIS SIMMACHIS
LIBER.V.EXPLICIT INCIPIT LIBER VI.
VE AB VRBE ROMA CONDITA AD CAPTAM VRBEM
tandem Romam sub regibus primũ. Consulibus dende. ac dic
taxoribus ⁊. urbsq ac tribunis consularibus gessore foris bella.
dom̃i seditiones quæ magno ex intuuallo loci uix comuniaur; tam
obscuras; uetus

plate x (a).   No. 88. Livy: subscription at the end of Bk. v.   Ms. Auct. T. i. 24, fol. 83ᵛ (detail).

quãillorum nos egritudinem capiamus; Pax audi quaesuperat
omnem mentem custodiat corda ura inxpoihu dñonostro/cuiest
gloria & potestas infecula feculorum. Amen
usque huc conotuli decoticae scae oelaviae nooov. EXPL.VII.
INCIPIT LIBER VIII
degraroivis vastaroione cuo parsen episcopus reotcerit.
uro laudabilem soluras ordinem? quid inpellras linguam legi
iustissime feruenram? quio prouocaras isermonem spus cedence?
quid inter mortoues capus festinaxas Aropedes? quio relinquetas
aaron producias eleazar? nonpaxor excludi forrem. &pro
fluere torrenrem solem abconoti? & stellam ostenroi? canroem
cedere? & inuenturem legis promulzaxpe sapiertram reoceye &im

plate x (b).   No. 89. Gregory of Nazianzus, Orations, tr. Rufinus: subscription at the end of vii.   Ms. Laud Misc. 276, fol. 63ʳ (detail).

poss. Sunt tam qdam qs nup pponunt. ut. at. ast aut. ac necneq; si quin queccapiut sin seu si
ue. ni. Aliae qs emp subponunt. ut. q; ne ue; q ctiam enclitices: quidem quoq; aut. quod
tam anti quisolebant etiam pponere. Aliae pene oms in differenc. et ppom et sub poni
possunt. ut. et atq; post ice pponunt. alias non. Ut ur g tn. u. u. suspiciens alti lunam et
sic uo ce peat. horatius in i. sermonum. cum me hortar etur par ce frugali atq; uiuere
uti contentu seo qd mihi ipse parasse. et e quide salte tam qua qua quando quarn? na enim
itaq; quo. qua ppt. ergo igit. et sciendu qd pler qq; coniunctiones quo modo p positiones
diuersas habent in una e eadem q; uoce significationes: qd in multis iam ostendimus. li
quoq; none pro mit tendum qd coniunctiones sibi p positę inueniunt ta eidem potest
tis cum sint quam alterius. Cicero in pg noscetis. Ast aut tenui q cand el lumine phacie
Virg in u. u. atq; e quide couert um memini si do nauenire. Ide in iii. Nam ne q; erat te poteta
astrorum ignes nec lucidus e ther sidera polus

PRISCIANI G PART ORATIONIS DE NOM LIB. VII.

DE VERBO LIB. III. DE PARTICIPIO LIB. I. DE PRO

NOM LIB. II. D EPPOSITIONE LIBER. I. DE ADVER

BIO ET INTERIECTIONE LIBER. I. DE CON

IUNCTIONE LIBER. I. EXPLICIUNT AM

FL THEODORUS DIONISII UIRI D M SS

E P ET ADIUTOR UM QUESTORIS. SCRIPSI MANU

ME ARTEM PRISCIANI UIRI DISERTISSIMI

GRAMMATICI DOCTORIS MEI IN URBE ROMA

CONSTANTINOPOLITANA DIE UKL

MARCII MAVORCIO UIRO CLARO

CONSULE XC PATRICIO.

tas· atq̃ in italia retentas· ēē· Hoc facto quãquam
nulli erat dubium quidnam contra cesarem parare
tur· tamen cesar omnia patienda ēē statuit· quoad
sibi spes aliqua relinqueretur· iure potius discep-
tandi quam belligerundi· contendit quadam
utra q̃ DIE FVTVRA·

IVLIVS CELSVS
CONSTANTIN' VC
LEGI TANV FELICIT,
CII ESARS POT MAX
EIMISRR CSR BLI
GLLC LIB· VIII· EPLICIT·

Usual readings, where they differ from
those first written on the patch:

uallis est disiunctus
ipsa contexta est. Sed haec
mantur (ratione) non sensu quaeren[dum]
seruauerit. Et Archi[medes]
quibus a terrae superficie luna
Venere, Mars a sole, a
stelliferum caelum omne spatium

gm̄ ppositiones aut ipsa uerba corrumpunt ut ficio· nā erat integru facio· aut
ipse corrumpunt ab integris uerbis ut adfero· nā erat integru fero· aut utruq;
& corrumpunt· & corrumpuntur ut afficio· nam affero qd scribebatur ur· p
x & d· incipit scribi per f· & x· & ut eundo exeat facio· hoc scio· prepo
sitio & quando pponitur· & quando post aponitur· sicut sensum suum retinet exceptā p̄po
sitione· utpote extensa· extra p· sicut cōsū mutat uestigium· sed ut aduer
bium· ut longo post tempore uenit· Ambigue p̄positiones· que quatuor
sunt· in· sub· super· & subter· ubi maiores indifferent urebant sed ho die
iam quesunt· in· & sub· hā· super· & subter· accusatiue habent· in aut· & qua
ratione seruentur in superiori tractatu est· pleruq; eade × prepositio·
quod est & aduerbium· quod ante & ppt· sed qd magis dicendu sit· hac ra
tione colligimus· & enim si pars orationis sequatur· que tasib; serus & p̄positio
nes erunt· ut ante templū ppt aquā· Templū eni & aquā· cōcusa eles par
tes orationis· quando aut· dicimus ante fecit· post dix aduerbia sunt·
sequantur eni uerba· & nouimus utiq; aduerbia sep uerbis egere· DE INT
interiectio × pars orationis· inter iecta aliis partib; ōrnis [LECTIONE·
ad exprimendos animi affectus· aut metuentis ut ei· aut optantis ut o·
aut dolentis ut heu· aut letantis· ut euax· sed hec aduerbiis greci
adplicant· qd ideo latini non faciunt· qa huiuscemodi uoces· non statim
sequitur uerbum· licet aut· p inter iectione etiā alias partes orationis
singulares· pluralesue subponere· ut nefas pnefas· Accentus int iec
tione certi est nonpossunt· ut fere in aliis uocib; quas inconditas inuenim̄
inter iectio nihil hab& · nisi solū mentis affectū· TRADITIO EIUSDEM
que tunc ū inter iectio dr· quando uoce incondita pfertur· O· heu & si
milia· Cir· aut· plenas adhibemus· ad exprimendos· animi affectus·
Nonna inter iectiones dīr· quā p inter iectionib; ut p iup prī ibit·
hic ait· & hec pars non potest pprium nom unius cuiusq; terre· eo qd
uarie inter iectiones sunt· Nam o· dolentis· legitur· ut o· mihi· p tex
tos referat· sic iup prter· Aut irascentis· ut o· callidos· homines & similia·
Barbarismus × una pars orationis [DE BARBARISMO
uitiosa· in cōmuni sermone· Impoematet· metaplas mus· Ideq; bar
baris mus· in nrā loque la· imperegrina· barbaro lexis dr· ut si quis
dicat· mastruca cera magalia· Barbaris mus fit duob; modis·
pnuntiatione & scripto· his bipartitis· quattuor species supponuntur·
Adiectio· detractio· Immutatio· transmutatio· Litte· syllabæ· tepe
tori· Aspirationis· p adiectione littæ fiunt barbarismi sic· ut relliquas
da naum· cū reliquas punu· l· diceredebeamus· syllabæ· ut nos abis exacti
p isse teporis· ut italiam fato pfugis· cū italiam correptā p malittera di
cere debeamus· p detractione littæ sic· ut infatib; p infantib; syllabæ ut
salmentū· p sacisamentū· teporis ut unius obnoxā· punius p in mutta

S

S

illic nec organa hydraulica sonant nec sub phonasco uocalium
concentus meditatum achroama simul intonat. nullus ibi
lyristes choraules mesochorus tympanistria psaltria canit.
rege solum illis fidib. delinito. quib. nonminus mulcet uirtus
animum quam cantus auditum. cum surrexerit inchoat
nocturnas aulica gaza custodias. armati regiae domus aditib.
assistunt. quib. horae primi soporis uigilabuntur. sed iam
quid meas istud ad partes quitibi indicanda nonmulta de
regno sed pauca de rege promisi. simul & stilo finem fieri
decet. quia & tu cognoscere uiri non amplius quam studia
personamq. uoluisti. & ego non historiam sed epistulam
efficere curaui.   UALE

SIDONIUS FILIMATIO SUO SALUTEM ·

Nunc & legis me ambitus interrogatum. senatumouem.
cur adipiscendae dignitati hereditariae curis per uigilib.
incumbam. cui pater socer auus proauus praefecturis urba
nis praetorianisq. magisteriis palatinis militaribus que
micuerunt. & ecce gaudentius meus hactenus tantum tri
bunicius. oscitantem nostrorum ciuium desidiam uicari
ano apice transcendit. mussitat quidem iuuenum nostro
rum calcata   nerositas   nsit clero
                        hoc solum mouetur ut gaudeat. Igitur
uenerantur huciusq. contemtum. ac subitae stupentes do
na fortunae. quem consessu despiciebant sede suspiciunt.

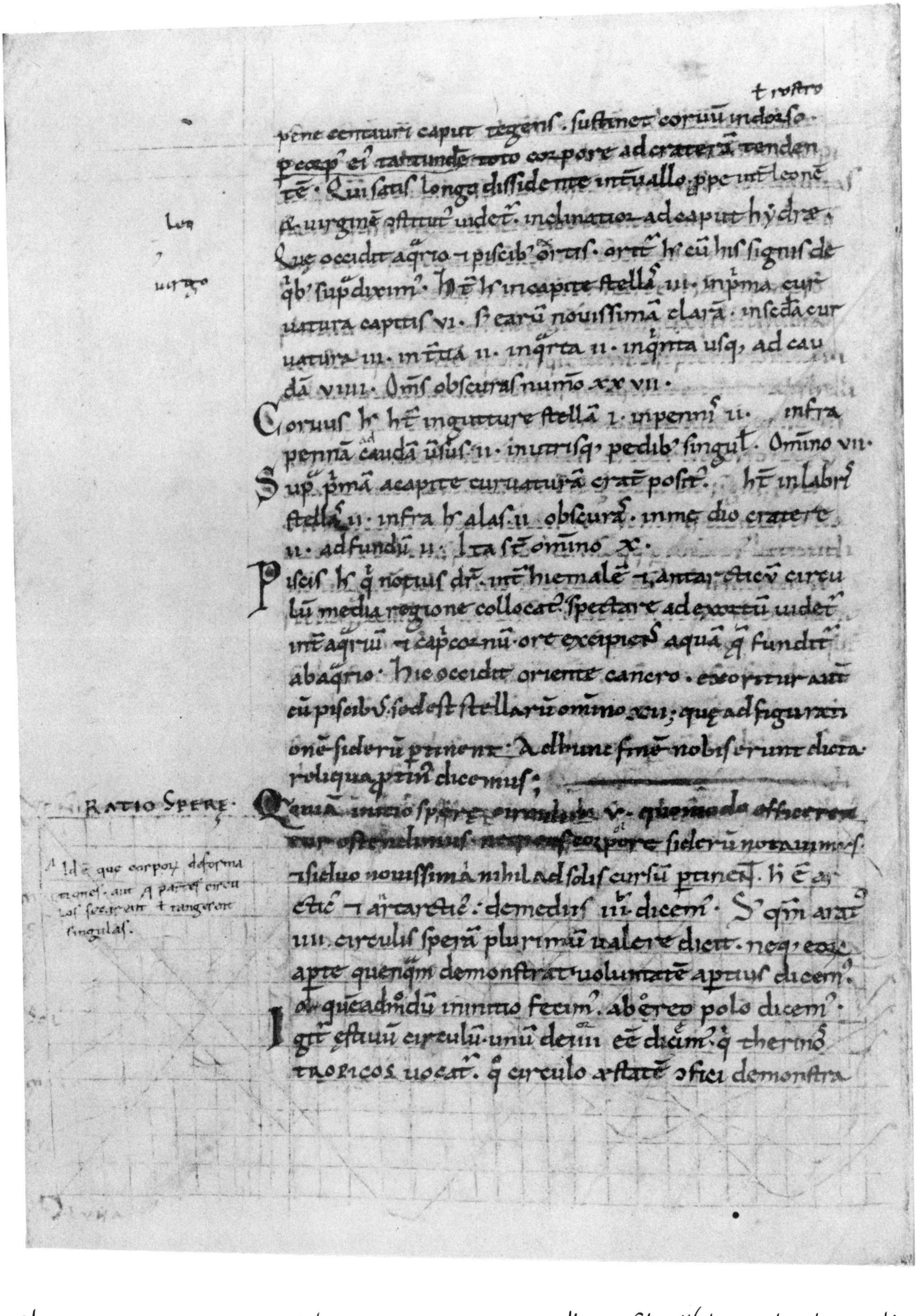

t rostro

Plate XVI.   No. 107. Palimpsest.   MS. D'Orville 95, fol. 28ᵛ (ultra-violet photograph).

Lower text: graph diagram illustrating the excerpt de cursu earum [sic, for planetarum]
per zodiacum circulum, from Pliny, Nat. Hist., II. 62, etc.

Upper text: Hyginus, Astronomica, III. 39 – IV. 1.

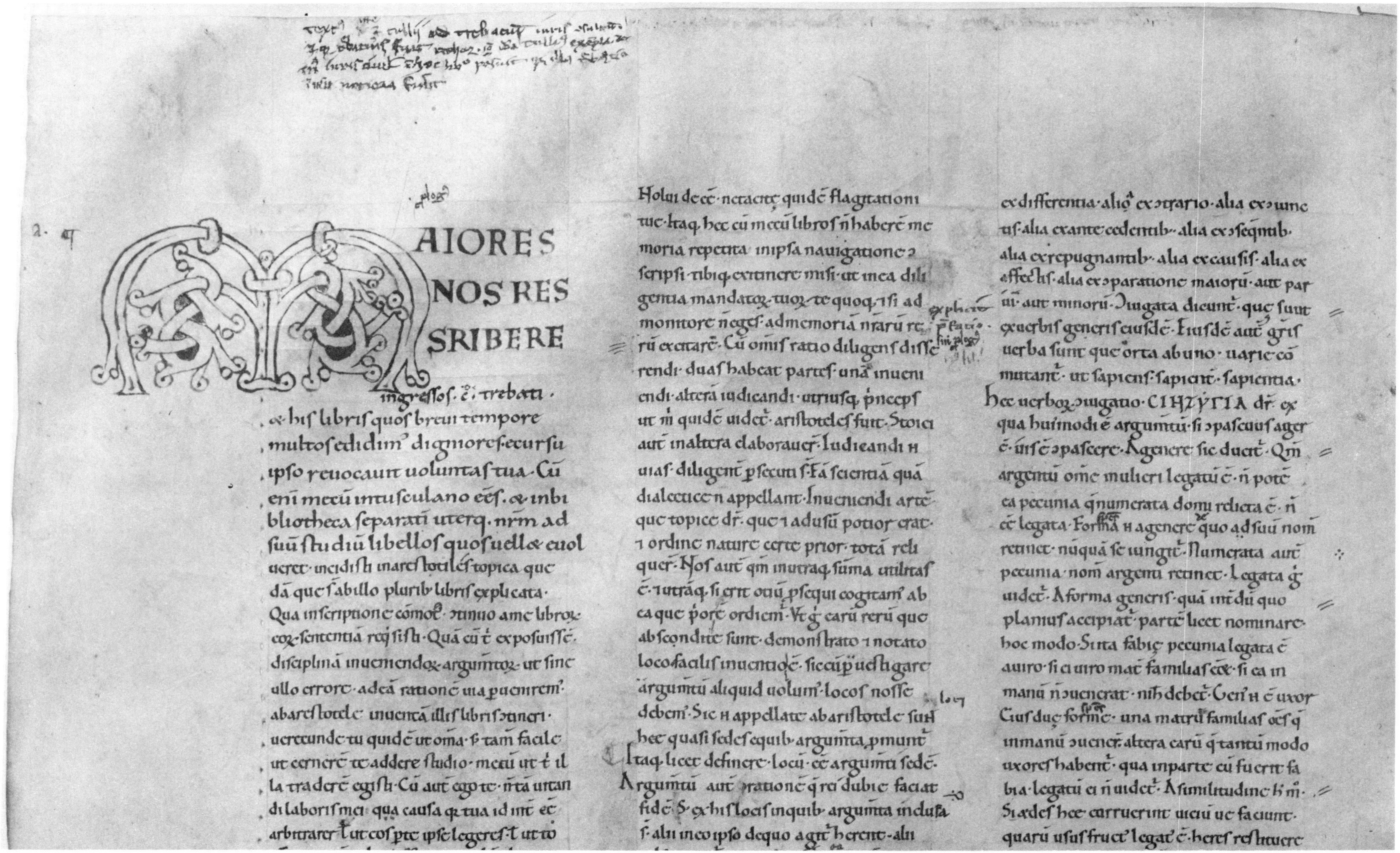

MS. Laud. Lat. 49, fol. 97ᵛ (top part).

Plate XVII.

No. 108. Cicero, Topica, beginning.

XVIII (a). No. 110.

Horace, _Odes_, II. xix, 24 – III. i, 18.

MS. D'Orville 158, fol. 17ʳ.

Plate XVIII (b). No. 111.

Horace, _Odes_, I. iii, 1–9.

Queen's Coll., MS. 202, part of fol. 5

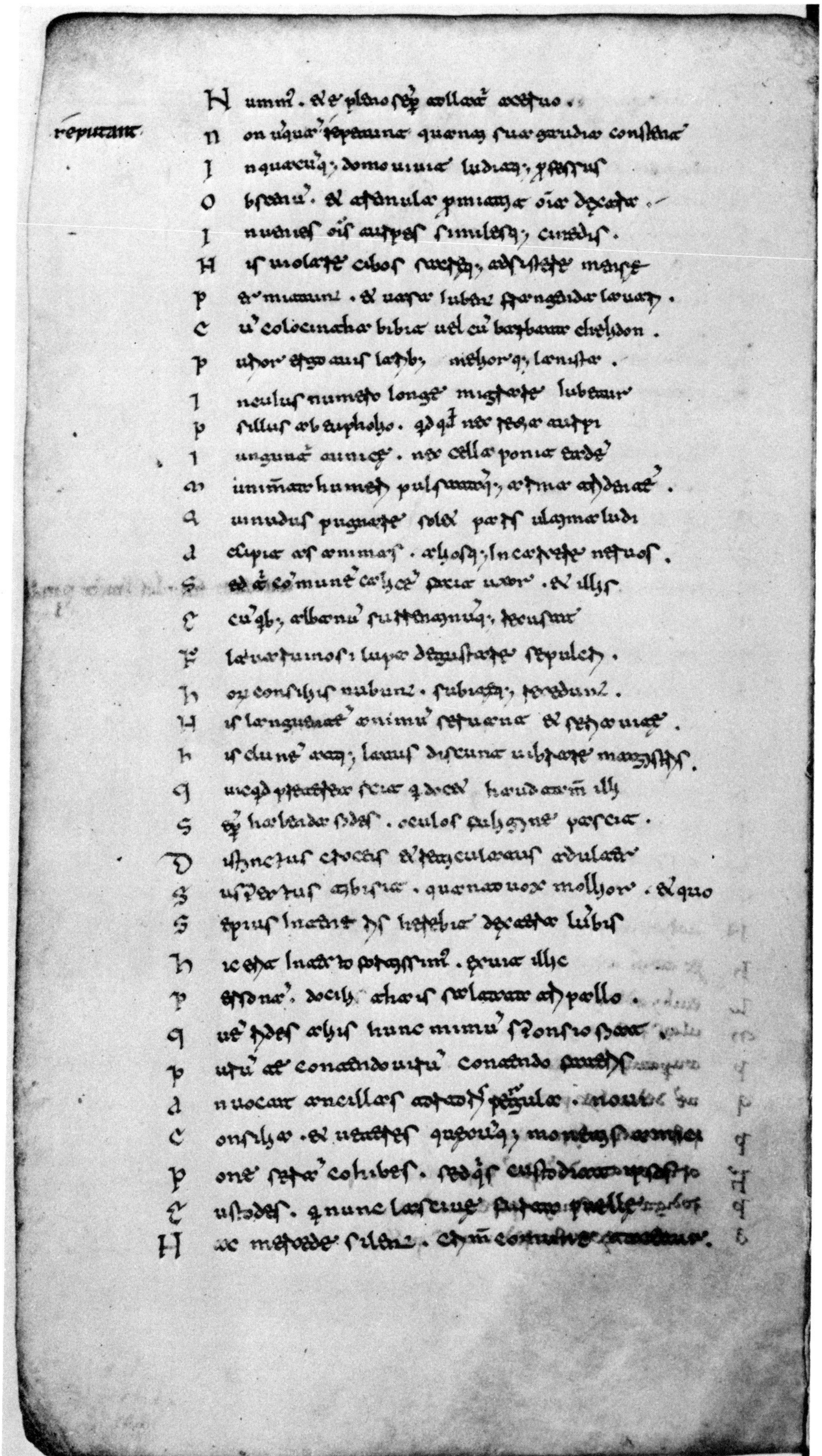

Plate XIX. No. 113. Juvenal, VI. 364–5 and lines 1–33 of the unique lines. MS. Canon. Class. Lat. 41, fol. 20ᵛ.

Plate xx(a).

No. 120. Glossary (letter A), in Latin and Old English, in the margin of Wulfstan the Cantor, *Narratio metrica de sancto Swithuno*, I.109–127.

MS. Auct. F.2.14, fol.11ʳ (top part).

(a)

Plate xx(b).

No. 116. Frontispiece to Cicero, *De inventione*: Cicero as consul hears the arguments of Cato 'Uticensis' and Caesar in deciding the fate of the Catilinarian conspirators.

MS. Barlow 40, fol.1ʳ.

(b)

pmansit. & diui augusti. atqᶻ adri
ani constitutionibus pcauetur ut
ē in mse. tā eqtes. qm pedites du
cāt ambulatim. Hoc eīn uerbo hoc
qᵈ exercitū nominant. Dece in
lia passuū armati instructiqᶻ ō
mibᵘ telis pedites. militari gradu
ire ac redire iubebant in castra.
ita ut & aliquā itineris parte cur
su alactiou efficerent. Eqtes n̄
diuisi ptinas armatiqᶻ similiter
tantū itineris pagebant. ita ut
equestre meditatione. intdū se
qnt̄. intdū cedant. & recursu qdā
impet repetent. Non solū aute
in cāpis. s̄; etiā in clinosis & arduis
locis. & descendē & ascendē utraqᶻ
acies cogebat. ut nulla ars uel ca
s̄; prlo pugnantibᵘ; posset accedē.
que non ante boni milites assidua
exercitatione didicissent.

b̄ec fidei ac deuotionis intu
itu imparor inuicte. deu
muersis auctoribᵘ; q rei militaris dis
ciplinā litis mandauerant. in hunc
libellū enuclea congessi. ut inde
lectu atqᶻ exercitatione tyronū
siqs diligens uelit existere: ad an
tique uirtutis imitatione facile cor
roborare possit exercitū. Necᶻ e
n̄ degenerauit in hominibᵘ mar
ti calor. nec effete s̄; ire que lace
demonios que athemenses que
marsos. que sēnites. que peligno
que ipsos pgenuere romanos. Ho
ne epirote armis plurimū aliqᵈo
ualuerint. Nonne macedones ac
tessali supatis psis. usqᶻ ad indiam
bellando penetrarunt? Dacos aut.
ce mesos. & traces. in tantū bellicosos
sep fuisse manifestū ē: ut ipsū mar
te fabule apud eos natū ē̄ confir
ment. Longū ē si omniū earū puin
ciarū uires enumerare contendā.

cū omnes in romani impii ditio
ne consistant. Sed longeua secu
ritas pacis. hommes parti ad dilec
tione otii. parti ad ciuilia trans
duxit officia. Ita cura exercitii mi
litaris pmo. neglegenti agi. pea
dissimulari. ac postremū olī mobli
uione pdita cognoscit. Nec aliqᵈ
hoc supiore etate accidisse mire
t̄: cū p pmū pumcū bellū. xx. aᶻ
qᵈ excurrit annoᵉ pax. ita roma
nos illos ubiqᶻ uictores. ocio & ar
moᵉ desuetudine eneruauerit.
ut sec̄o pumco bello. hannibali
pares ē̄ n̄ possent. Tot itaqᶻ;
consulibᵘ. tot ducibᵘ; tot exercitibᵘ
dimissis. tā demū aduictoriā p
ueuerunt: cū usū exercituꝗᶻ
militarē condiscere potuerunt.
Seper q legendi. & exercendi sē
tirones. Ita uti eni constat. eru
dire armis suos. quā alienos mer
cede conducere. Flauii Vegetii
Renati. uiri illustris de
Re militari liber .I.
Ad Imparorem Theodo
sium explicit. Incipiunt
capitula libri Secundi.

I n̄ quo genere diuidat res militaris.
Q uid int̄ legiones & auxilia int̄ sit.
Q ua causa exhauriri fecerit legiones.
Q uotas legiones antiq ad bellū duxerut.
Q uē admodū llegio constituatur.
Q uot cohortes sit in una legione qt̄ milites
in una cohorte sint.
N omina itachns pncipū legionis.
N omina eoᵉ q antiqs ordines dixeret.
D e officio pfecti legionis.
D e officio pfecti castroᵉ.
D e officio pfecti fabroᵉ.
D e officio tribuni militū.
D e censuis qugillis peditum.
D e tmis eqtū legionarioᵉ.
Q uē admodū legionū acies instruatur.

Plate XXI.   Lincoln College, MS. Lat. 100, fol. 9ʳ.

No.125. Vegetius, Epitoma rei militaris, I. 27-28, & capitula to Bk. II.

No. 132. Pliny the Elder, *Naturalis Historia*, beginning of Bk. II.

New College, MS. 274, fol. 9r.

Plate XXII.

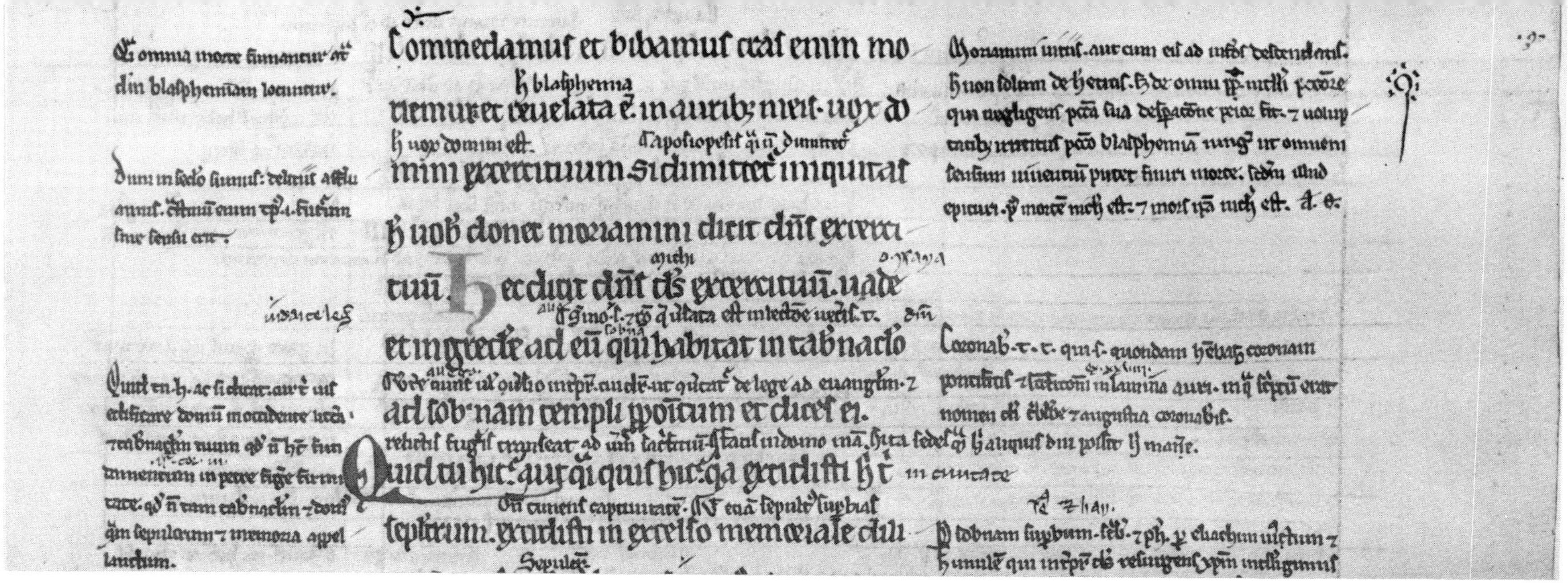

Top of page.

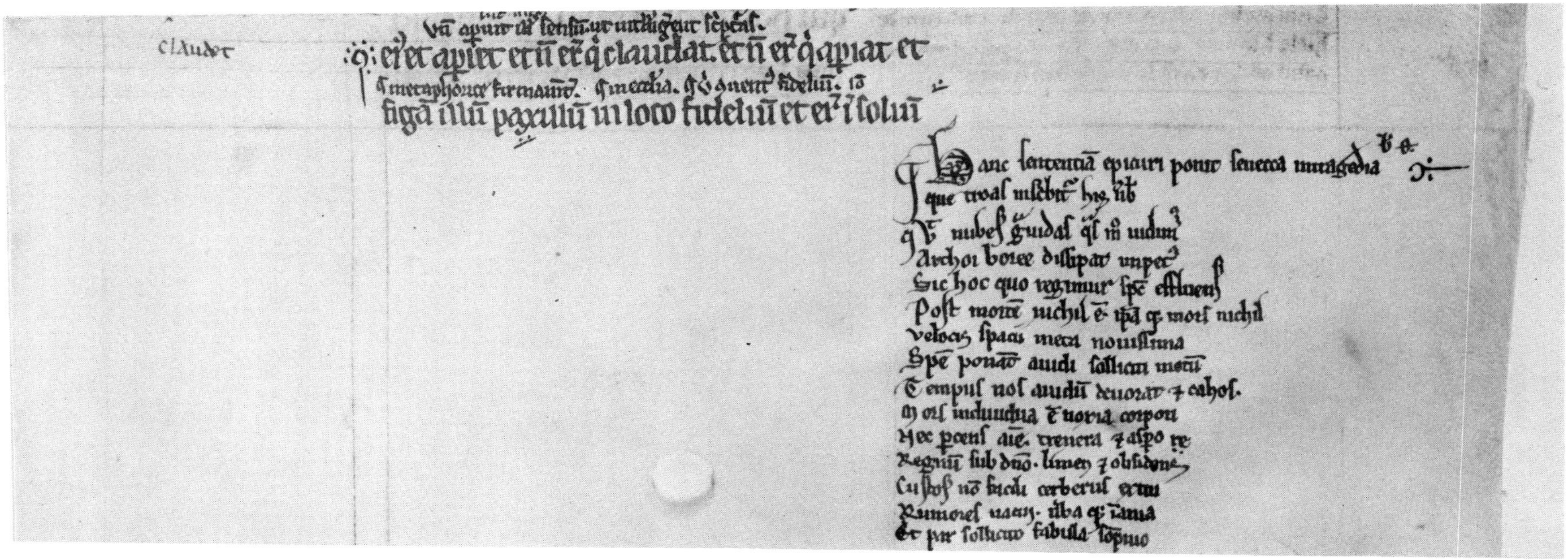

Bottom of page.

Plate XXIII. No. 134. Seneca, Troades, 394–406, quoted as a gloss to Isaiah xxii. 13. New College, MS. 21, fol. 31r.

Cicero Varroni salutem. Ex iis litteris quas Atticus a te missas mihi legit, quid ageres et ubi esses cognoui. Quando autem te uisuri essemus, nihil sane ex iisdem litteris potui suspicari. In spem tamen uenio appropinquare tuum aduentum. Et mihi est solacio, sed tamen ita est ut rebus urgentibus nullam alleuationem afferat. Dissimillimi sunt enim rerum publicarum, tamen ea potius mihi ante oculos uersantur quam illa quae minant. Ego sic tecum enim me postea quam urbem uenerim te uideo cum ueteribus amicis, ad te iam uenturum nihil peregrinum et sui ideo cor nostro demensa. Ad huius sententia est et ad cor me sub praeterito.

Videbam enim in eis me inter ambulationem sociis ... illorum si ... et parum est ignoscendum in reuocato ... et consuetudine sua ... te ... quod meo perseuerat sapientiorem quam me diceres fuisse una obser uare ... placet insuetior uideret ... sit te interim ea ... et ... impediat me facile senatus. Quamobrem siue deam ... siue remaneam placebit siue ... roma ... sunt ... iam ... quo modo sum ... ut esse compromittas.

Cicero Varroni. Cum iam ... mihi cum ad me ... uenit et in posterum die mane ad te iterum ... dixisti. Dixit me ... ad ... rogaui ut ... epistulam non ... ille ad me nec ille ad me redisset obliti ... credit ... et ... non epistulam misisti per meos si mediisset ex eode... pridie mane et in ... ad ... reperito priuatis ... diebus ... nimine expectarem ... uento ... mane ... ad te statim ... et si eum ... illa ... epistula praesertim ... postea nobis ... a ... tamen ... meo notum et ... in animo eo ... homine ... et ...

... ea sui ... ad te ...

... uobis autem ... consilium ... subinui ... interim oculos hominum ... neque nunc ... te publici. Cum enim uictoria te ... uictos nos inuenire ... modo ... nos colere inuicem et res fortasse ... si ... tum non obstat huiusmodi ... quae tu ... et tui ... prudentia inuicem omnia credo ... te eximio te fellit ... et tamen ... cum maioris teneret ... offerret ... unam securitatem ad id quidem uis prudens uel momentum belli ... et aliis ... iubea quam agebamus ... dicebamus ... uidere nec audire si ... aestimabat ... turbabat qui obuiam in uenisset ut cuius ... ait suspicatus aut dicturus et si non suspicit ... pro se aut metuit et ea relegit aliquid obscurum ... et ... uana ... deinde temeritate suspicatur et qui fortasse me oportet ... puto me ... dico et quidem homines oculi mei terro non ... et eo ... suspicans ad id uenit et tamen. Cum hac et me consuetudo ... calumniam ... stomacho meo ... rationem consilii mei ... censeo ... tantum ... dum ... et ... haec ... et ... si uiderint ... quemadmodum negotium confectum sit. Confectum cum epistola magna ... uidero qui ... uictoris animus qui ... uero ... uno me ... ducat ... sed experto tamen si te uolo si ipse ... iam ... ut ad ... uenire cum tamen ... nobis honesti... et cum hic ... uideri uel ... in ... loca ... natam. Sed eo tu melius nobis in ul timo uia ... uult ... uero etiam salutem non dextre si ... uolet quod modo ... uult etiam ut ... ad conseruandam te publicam ... libens occurrit si nemo inter...

et libro quidem hoc continentur epistolae Ciceronis ad Varronem et quosdam alios.

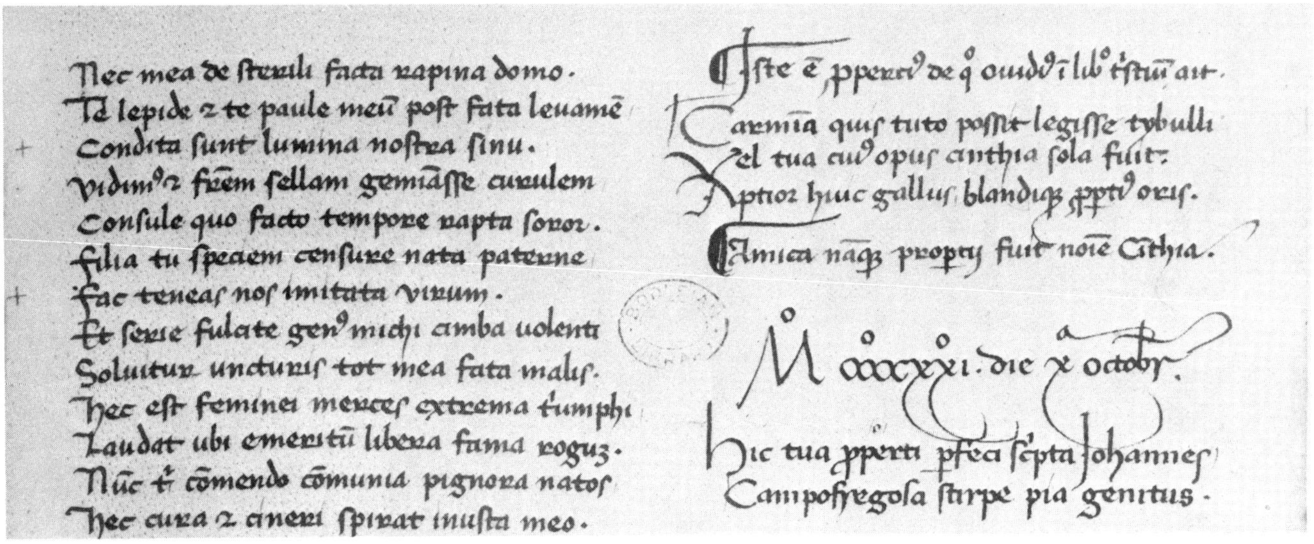

Plate XXV(a). No. 144. Propertius, IV. xi, 62–74, and colophon. MS. Holkham Misc. 36, fol. 17r (top).

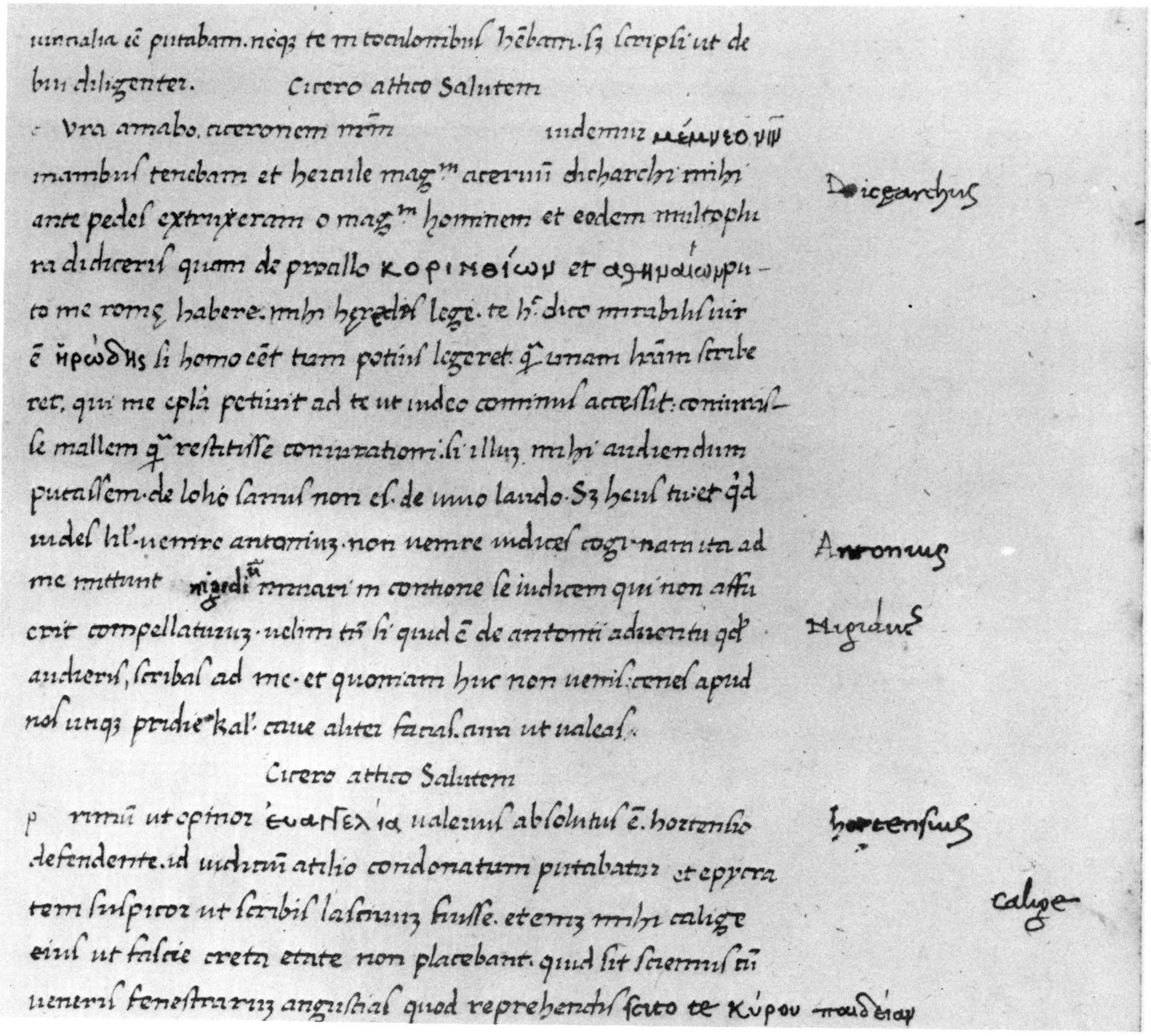

Plate XXV(b). No. 145. Cicero, Epistulae ad Atticum, II. i, 12 – iii, 2. MS. Lat. class. c. 7, fol. 70r (top).

matri uacare solite erant. has ap
pollo colligauit ae stabiles fec
Septem montes urb rome.
Tarpeius. Esquilinus. palatinus.
Celius. Auentinus. Quirinalis.
Viminalis. Nunc nomina q̃u
cumq; usibus eterne urbis for
may confluctionibus auecte s.
iudicemus.
Claudia inuenta ae adducta e
a Claudio cesare.
Martia inueta e a marco Agrippa
Traiana inuenta adductaq; e
a Traiano Augusto.
Tepula ite a marco Agrippa in
uenta deductaq; est t.
Iulia inuenta ab Aureliano
perductaq; est t.
Alsiatina item inueta perductaq;
est a Claudio cesare.
Alexandriana inuenta pductaq;
e ab Alexandro.
Virgo inuenta est deductaq; e
ab Agrippa cesare.
Drusia inuenta perductaq; est
a Druso.
Preter hec replet̃ aeia indige
nis nimphis que ammiratur
uirgo enea talit italiam dyxat.

Nymphe laurentes. Nymphe gen
amnibus unde e.
INCIPIT PROLOGVS DE MEN
SVRA ORBIS TERRE.
Post congregata eptam de
questionibus dece artis gra
matice cogitaui ut liber de men
sura prouintiay orbis terre se
q̃retur sedm illoy aũctem q̃s
fuit Theodosius imperator ad
prouintias pdictas mensuradas
miserat. Et iuxta pliniu scdi
predata aũcte ỹaỹ dimissio
nem uolo supplens ondere S;
duabz causis cont tepoy roein
scriptura missoy theodosii uer
bis plinii scdi ordine scribedi
ppono eo qd illi in duodenis
nouissime uersibz diligetius
antiquis feasse affirmant ae
qd exemplaria codici natalis
historie plinii scandi q scru
tatus sui nimis a scriptoribz
ultimoy tepoy dissipata pindi.
Sermones quide pdictoy missoy
qa min uitiose scripti sr q̃tr
potuero corrigere curabo. At
ubi in libris plinii scandi cor
ruptis absq; dubio numeros

.Theodosius.

P. Linius scdi

Select index of names
The numerals refer to item numbers.

Addenda et Corrigenda

No.

59. Illegible parts of this manuscript were treated with galls, probably for the benefit of Richard Bentley, see Exh. Cat., *Richard Bentley, a tercentenary exhibition*, Brotherton Library, University of Leeds, 1962, no. 3.

85. The hand of the Ps.-Apollodorus, exhibited, is the same as that in pl. 64 (b) of D. Harlfinger, *Specimina griechischer Kopisten der Renaissance, I Griechen des 15. Jahrhunderts*, Berlin 1974 (the name of the copyist is not known; both books belonged to Bessarion).

107. (End of the first paragraph): for 103, fol. 33^v read 103, fol. 34^r.

131. (Bibliography): for Colkes read Colker.

162. Mr. M. D. Reeve has kindly pointed out that Ferrarius' additions are made in two sorts of ink: those marked as from the 'old codex' are in a darker shade; the additions in the lighter shade, not so marked, include lines supplied by 15th-cent. humanists.

Appendix to no. 130: the household of an unidentified 14th-cent. ecclesiastical dignitary.

Merton College, MS. 311, fol. 100ᵛ

Ih(es)u m(aria) P.L.W.C. L.A. o. s(an)c(t)i m.

[col.i]   clerici

ꝶ. magister Ricꝯ.
      B(ar)tolinus
      Galacius
      Reynerius
      Felicianus
      Bartho(lo)m(eus) camerarius

              domicelli
      Beaumond (?)
      Chilke
      Attiman· (?)
      Monald
      Lonne (?)
      Sant touch
      Peryn
      Fredericus corꝯ
      Vitulun (?)· domicellus domini Ricꝯ
      domicellus Bartholini
      Dyne nepos Iohannis de flo.
                    rencia. clericus

[col.ii]   fratres
      frater Willelmus
      frater Gerardus socius
           minores
      frater Angelus
      frater Guido alñ capellanus

frater Moyl (?)   [col.ii continued]
frater Anton

         Camerarii
Iohannes de Florencia
Thomas ia. uel Masseleñ.
Bon Joh(a)n
Reynald' lector in mensa

              clericus domini Ric̄ Pet(ro)cius

         Garc̄ones in panetria et hotelaria
Van socius Rogeri Rogerius
Ianitor Vaynol (?)
                            Ianoch nuntius
Reynerius
         In stabulo
Ianoch palefridarius
Henrꝯ palefridarius
Gerard Capoī palefridarius
Magister Iohannes liberator prebende
Gerardus liberator fo(ra)minis (?)
Comite ~~palefridarius~~ [deleted]
Nich custos equorum aliorum a palefrid
Ianoch garc̄. Chilke
         In coquina
Vite ⎤ pagii
Peroch' ⎦